In Memoriam

This book is acknowledged and dedicated to the memory of the late Shadrack Yaak Deng Akoy, the founding president of the Twi East Community Association of Australia Inc.

This is the first published book by Twi East Community Association of Australia Inc.
TECAA 2019 AGM Conference and Reunion Complied Report.
Melbourne, Victoria, Australia
© TECAA Inc. No. 1601085 ABN 11 326 116 868

No part of this report may be reproduced by any means without permission from TECAA management. Requests and enquiries regarding reproduction should be addressed to:
TWI EAST COMMUNITY ASSOCIATION OF AUSTRALIA
Email: twicommunityassociation-au@outlook.com
Facebook: Twi East Community Association of Australia Website: www.tecaa.au.org
Inc. No. 1601085 ABN 11 326 116 868

The Australia Incorporation Act protects this material.

Please note:

While all care has been taken in the preparation of this book, no responsibility is accepted by the TECAA management and Compiler for any errors, omissions, or inaccuracies. The material provided in this book has been prepared to provide general information discussed during the 2019 TECAA AGM, Conference and Reunion in Melbourne. It is not intended to be relied upon as or to be a substitute for legal or other professional advice. No responsibility can be accepted by the Compiler or Executive for any known or unknown consequences that may result from reliance on any information provided in this publication.

Final document sent to TECAA Management on 18 April 2020
First published December 2020.

ISBN: 9780645010299

Disclaimer:

The organizing committee has endeavored to record all information presented during the TECAA 2019 Conference in the manner and form in which they were presented. Every effort has been made to ensure that information contained in this publication is as accurate as possible. To the best of our knowledge, the published material is correct and up to date at the time of publication (December 2020). Reports of speeches attributed to certain speakers are not printed verbatim. Photographic material presented in this booklet is illustrative only and does not imply any endorsements whatsoever. This publication is a summation of the 2019 TECAA AGM and Conference and does not purport to contain every piece of information about the proceedings of the conference. Detailed information is available in the audio-visual recordings of the proceedings and in the event minutes. This conference report is for TECAA, its members, and affiliated organizations. It may be obtained for free by members of TECAA with prior authorization by TECAA leadership.

Table of Contents

Foreword	v
Acknowledgments	vii
Dedication	ix
Part A: Executive Summary And Introduction	1
Executive summary	1
Introduction	3
Objectives of Conference	4
Report Outline	7
Part B: Welcoming Of Delegation And Members Into The Conference	8
Part C: The Agm & Progress Report From The President	11
Achievements	11
Challenges	13
Appreciations and Introductions	13
Discussions: Q & A Session:	14
Conclusion of AGM Session	15
Part D: Research And Presentations Session	17
Sustainable Development	18
Why Return to Twi Land is Rational and Feasible	23
The Resources Available and the Education and Knowledge Required to Capitalise on Them	29
Conflict Management	33
Setting a Foundation for Healthy Community	35
Organizational Success and Challenges	42
Part E: Speeches And Discussions	45
Keynote Address 1: Philip Aguer Panyang (Former Governor of Jonglei State)	45
Keynote Address 2: Hon. Isaiah Chol Aruai	48
Keynote Address 3: Ayiei Manyok Ajak	51
Keynote Address 4: Mr. Benjamin Bul Duom (Chair of Council of Elders)	53
Keynote Address 5: Mr. Ajang Diing Awuol (Twi East Youth Leader, Juba)	54
Keynote Address 6: States/Territory Leaders' Representative	55
Keynote Address 7: County Representatives	55
Keynote Address 8: Akech Dau Angok	56
Keynote Address 9	57
Part F: Viewpoints	58
Part G: Appendix	62
Appendix A) Conference Evaluation Form	62
Evalutation Summary	63
Appendix B) The Discussion Form	64
Proposals	65
Appendix C) Attendance Lists	66
Appendix D) The Conference Research Paper Processes	71
Appendix E) Name Tag Policy	72
Appendix F) The Order Of Proceedings In The Event Proceedings	73
Appendix G) TECAA Invitation Letter	75
Appendix H) Appreciation Letter	75

Foreword

Deng Chol Riak
TECAA President

Members of TECAA are proud of their roots in Twi land. They formed this association to marshal their human and financial resources for furthering the development of their community. Accordingly, 'service to the people' is their various invaluable supports have been given to TECAA since its inception in 2009.

The critical mission of the past, present, and future of TECAA is to appropriately identify, utilize, and allocate the resources for the benefit of the community-that is, to improve the living conditions of Twi people.

At home, the Twi community faces multifaceted threats, including insecurity caused by hostile neighboring communities; flooding from the overflowed White Nile; food insecurity caused by environmental conditions, as well as issues of personal insecurity and safety, affecting farming; lack of reliable transport (impassable dirt roads and tracks); limited communication technologies, inadequate health and education services; lack of important social amenities; depopulation caused by migration and displacement due to past and ongoing civil wars; socioeconomic disruptions caused by prolonged civil wars; and weakened institutions of traditional governance, just to name a few. These are difficult challenges. Twi people at home and in the diaspora must, therefore, join hands to deal with these problems.

The 2019 TECAA Reunion Conference, which focused on the theme of New Approach + New Ideas = Supporting Progress, inspired hope of finding solutions to these problems.

The conference offered TECAA members opportunities for genuine discourse on issues important to the life and progress of their organization and community. The resources presented in this publication will help members of TECAA to be informed, empowered, and engaged. This 2019 conference booklet will be a useful companion for all members and leaders of this great Twi community.

Acknowledgements

Theme: New Approach + New Ideas = Supporting Progress
Report compiled by David Dau Deng

On behalf of the organizing committee, I wholeheartedly appreciate the support and the love you all have demonstrated throughout this process. I sincerely acknowledge and appreciate the enormous generosity, support, and assistance offered by the following people and organizations:

- I want to thank the TECAA Executive Committee, led by Deng Chol Riak, for entrusting me with the design, planning, coordination, and facilitation of the 2019 TECAA conference and for assigning me to compile the conference report. I acknowledge the technical support provided by members of the event management committee, advisory board, and Council of Elders.
- A special thanks goes to all members of the Twi community, especially the leaders of states, territories, Payams, and clans (sub communities or sections), for their invaluable support of the 2019 TECAA AGM and Conference. I want to unreservedly thank the host state of Victoria, led by Peter Akol Dhiak Akol, for hosting one of TECAA's best conferences.
- I want to give thanks to the researchers and keynote speakers who shared their expertise, knowledge, and wisdom during the conference. They charted a path and provided a springboard for TECAA to rely on moving forward.
- Thank you to all of our distinguished guests and delegates who traveled from South Sudan and East Africa for the conference to offer their time and contribution. The guest speaker and head of the delegation, Philip Aguer Panyang Jot, the former governor of Jonglei State, provided great insights during the conference, and we want to thank him for sharing his vast knowledge and experience.
- I am greatly indebted to all members of the Twi community. To the women and men of all ages who turned out in record numbers for the conference, and to those who tuned into the social media livestream, you all made the 2019 TECAA Conference a colorful and lively event! And to all those who completed evaluation forms and provided vital feedback on the proceedings of the 2019 TECAA Conference, thank you. The suggestions provided will be used to improve future conferences.
- I also want to thank Akech Ador, who livestreamed the conference to reach global audiences, and Maketh Bul of JB Production, who provided magnificent photography and videography of the event.
- Last but not the least, I want to sincerely thank Diing Bul Atem and Peter Garang Kuir for helping to edit this report. I thank them for invaluable suggestions on the structure and formatting of this publication. Like many people in our community, these gentlemen are often very busy, but for the love of this community, they took time out of their busy schedule to help put this document together.
- Again, I would like to congratulate previous leaders for succinctly setting out the objectives to meet current barriers.

I hope you will enjoy the readings of this booklet.

TECAA 2019 Conference Organizer, Consultant, And Report Compiler.

David Dau Deng is TECAA's current advisor on culture and community development. He is, the founding president of the Sudanese Community Association in the ACT, and the former relief and supplier coordinator in SRRA at Lobone 1 Displaced Camp. He has also held many other positions in the community sector. David holds a Master of Commerce, a Bachelor of Business, and a number of other certificates. He has worked in different levels of government in Australian, Commonwealth, state, and government agencies, and he has extensive experience in managing the Incorporated Association.

Dedication

The Twi East Community Association of Australia Inc. (TECAA) would not have been possible without the devotion of its past leaders, the late Shadrack Yaak Deng Akoy, Mangar Ayuel Malual, and Kuer Dau Apai, and without the continuing efforts of its current leadership. We would like to thank the president of TECAA, Deng Chol Riak, and his team for pursuing, with the utmost enthusiasm, the objectives for which this great organization was formed. The contribution of members of TECAA has been more than inspirational.

x

Part A: Executive Summary And Introduction

Executive Summary

The Twi East Community Association of Australia Inc. (TECAA) was founded just over a decade ago by members of the Twi East community living in Australia, across all the states and territories. Almost all of these founding members were proud Australian citizens. They formed the organisation as a forum for advancing their common interests and welfare in Australia and globally.

The Twi East Community Association of Australia Inc. held a reunion conference under the theme of New Approach + New Ideas = Supporting Progress in Melbourne on 20 and 21 September 2019 to chart a new path for the people of the Twi East community in Australia and around the world. This was the second global conference by the association and was attended by nearly a thousand people, including local organisation members and invited delegates from South Sudan and East Africa.

Over the course of the two-day event, conference participants discussed a range of topics related to health and wellbeing, education, organisation development and strategy, and sustainable socioeconomic development. During the conference, some attendees presented research papers, shared expert opinions, provided suggestions, and presented insightful analyses for consideration by the association. The conference program was divided into three parts: a progress report from the president of the association, followed by short discussions and a question and answer session; presentations by invited scholars; and finally, presentations by selected keynote speakers from the Twi East community and international delegates (also of Twi East community).

The delegation from South Sudan and East Africa, led by former Governor Philip Aguer Panyang, included Hon Isaiah Chol Aruai, commissioner of the South Sudan National Bureau of Census and Statistics; Hon Ayiei Manyok Ajak, commissioner of Jonglei State Revenue Authority and former MP of Pakeer Constituency; Ajang Diing Awuol, Twi East Youth Leader in Juba; Sultan Chol Dau Barach, chief of Panwiir clan of the Ayual community of the Twi Central County of Jonglei State; Hon Kuir Dau Kuir, former director of the Norwegian People's Aid (NPA), South Sudan; Nhial Garang Ageer, former leader of the Red Army and former chairman of phase two of the Kakuma Refugee Camp; Rev Peter Garang Deng Adit, general secretary of the Twi East Diocese; and Aguer Bol Kuir, a member of leadership for Twi East Youth in Juba.

Executives of the Day

Gabriel G. Juach
TECAA V. President

Ayiik C. Anyang
TECAA S/General

Deng C. Riak
TECAA President

Akoi B.

Lual A.

Majok L.

Mamer Y.

We are very thankful and very appreciative to Twi Community Members

Introduction

As soon as they ascended into office, TECAA's new Executive Committee began to organise a reunion conference for all members of the Twi East community in Australia and across the globe. Invitations were sent to selected would-be delegates from the Twi East community in different parts of the world. Some notable community leaders from the Twi East community, mainly from Africa, accepted the invitations and attended the Melbourne reunion conference. The conference was also attended by almost a thousand community members from within Australia.

The responsibility of organising this momentous event was assigned to an independent organising committee called the Event Management Committee (EMC), which was led by David Dau Deng, the current advisor for culture and community development at TECAA, designated as the chief event manager and consultant. The organising committee was instructed to design, plan, coordinate, and facilitate a two-day TECAA conference in Melbourne, Australia. Akoi Bol Nyuon, a member of the TECAA Executive Committee, was appointed as a special rapporteur to assist David Dau Deng and the organising committee, or event management committee (EMC).

There were three subcommittees that worked in conjunction with the EMC to ensure the conference was conducted efficiently. These were the finance and budget subcommittee, the communication subcommittee, and the hosting subcommittee. The finance and budget subcommittee, led by TECAA treasurer Mamer Yaak Dut and assisted by Lual Akoy, was responsible for procuring finances for the conference, which were sourced by soliciting funds through funding, contributions, and sponsorships. This subcommittee was also responsible for producing accurate recordings of all conference-related expenses and financial reports. It was supervised by TECAA president Deng Chol Riak. The communication subcommittee was headed by TECAA Secretary General Ayiik Chol Anyang and was assisted by TECAA Secretary for Information Majok Lual. The communication subcommittee was responsible for disseminating conference-related information, marketing and promoting the conference, and managing conference attendance by registering and issuing nametags to all conference attendees. Lastly, the hosting subcommittee was led by Peter Akol Dhiak Akol, the chairperson of the Twi East Community Association in Victoria Inc., which is an affiliate of TECAA. This subcommittee was responsible for all conference hosting needs, including procuring a suitable venue, making arrangements for seating and furnishings, ushering guests, and catering.

To meet the objectives of the conference, the EMC selected a series of topics for discussion during the event. The topics were assigned to selected members (who are experts in their fields) of the Twi community, who researched their assigned topics and presented their findings during the conference. These topics were selected based on identified needs or challenges in the community and on anticipated benefits of discussion. Furthermore, the EMC also identified keynote speakers, the majority of whom were members of a delegation from South Sudan and East Africa, to attend the conference. The first day of the conference, 20 September 2019, was restricted to members of the Twi community, including international delegates. But on the second day of the conference, invited guests from our sisterly communities of Duk, Bor, and other South Sudanese communities were able to attend.

The Objectives of the Conference

The 2019 TECAA conference was a monumental undertaking. It brought together members of the Twi community in Australia and from home, offering them a roundtable to discuss serious issues affecting their community and to propose solutions to these issues. It charted credible pathways for TECAA, re- energized the leadership team, and refined and synchronized various policy frameworks. It also offered members a platform to engage with their association, sharing knowledge and expertise, forging new working relationships, and exchanging problem-solving best practices. Similarly, the conference presented the community with an opportunity to celebrate a get-together, or reunion, of its members scattered around the globe. The conference, lauded as one of a kind, was a great display of Twi's spirit of ingenuity.

The principal objective of the conference was to explore better ways to deliver quality services to the people of the Twi community. The 2019 TECAA conference was the second largest gathering held by TECAA since its inception. The main objectives of the conference were framed around general themes or identified issues affecting the community. Objectives included:

- To identify and address issues affecting the Twi East community in Australia and back home. These include:
- Insecurity caused by hostile neighboring communities;
- Floods from the overflowed White Nile;
- Food insecurity as a consequence of ongoing insecurity; o Lack of reliable means of transportation (impassable dirt roads or tracks);
- Limited communication and information technologies;
- Inadequate health and education services;
- Lack of other social amenities;
- Depopulation and displacement due to past and ongoing civil wars;
- Socioeconomic disruptions;
- Weakened institutions of traditional governance.
- To bring together members of the Twi East community from across the globe to foster social interactions.
- To provide a platform for sharing ideas and discussing ways to resolve issues affecting members of our community. § To offer all participants an opportunity to voice their concerns and suggest solutions by promoting consensus around common ideas and strategies.

In this photo are the state leaders:
- Mr. Akol Ziak of Victoria
- Mr. Majok Jawat of WA
- Mr. Nuul Mayen of NSW
- Mr. Chut Aleer of ACT

Rev Samuel K. Majok and Conan Mark A. Thuch

'South Sudan is one of the richest places on Earth. Its wealth consists of vast arable land, generous rainfall, rich flora and fauna, and good, patient people who would die in defense of their dignity and humanity.'

Atem Y. Atem

The Report Outline

This conference report is comprised of eight parts:
- Part A covers the summary and general introduction of the conference;
- Part B deals with the reports of the AGM and its Q&A session;
- Part C presents the research topics addressed and presentations made by invited researchers;
- Part D covers keynote speeches from the delegates and distinguished members of the community; o Part E covers speeches from prominent members of our community;
- Part F concludes and summarises the outcomes of the conference;
- Part G compiles feedback and survey materials;
- Part H compiles the appendices, which include attendance lists, evaluation forms, discussion forms, processes for research papers, and conference programs, as well as the nametag policy, a sample invitation letter, a sample appreciation letter, TECAA's population pie chart, and TECAA's conference flyer.

Part B: Welcoming of Delegates and Members to the Conference

The 2019 Twi East Community Association of Australia Inc. (TECAA) Conference brought together global members of the Twi East community. The leader of the host state of Victoria, Peter Akol Dhiak Akol, extended a warm welcome to the delegation, led by former governor of Jonglei State Hon Philip Aguer Panyang Jot, and to all members of the Twi East community in attendance. He expressed his sincere gratitude to the Twi people in Victoria who had worked hard to provide accommodation and transport to members of our community who came from interstate or from Africa for the conference.

Peter Akol Dhiak also thanked TECAA leaders, past and present, for organizing the community into a vibrant association. He acknowledged efforts made by the entire membership of the Twi community to put together such an extraordinary event. He urged members to cultivate unity of purpose to advance the interests of the Twi

community. He also encouraged cooperation among various levels of Twi leadership to move the community forward in a purposeful and fruitful manner. To conclude his welcome, he heartily thanked all the conference attendees, expressing his pride in being the leader of the Twi community in the state of Victoria.

The final act of welcoming was performed by Gabriel Garang Juach, the deputy president of TECAA. He welcomed and introduced 10 members of the delegation to the conference.

- Hon Philip Aguer Panyang Jot, former governor of Jonglei State, South Sudan; a former spokesperson of South Sudan's national army, the SPLA; and a former director of SSRA, based in Panyagoor. Hon Philip Aguer was the head of delegation.
- Hon Isaiah Chol Aruai, a former (first) commissioner of Twi East County, Jonglei State; a commissioner of South Sudan's National Bureau of Census and Statistics, and a chairperson of Kongor Development Association (KONDA);
- Hon Ayiei Manyok Ayiei, a former MP in the Jonglei State parliament and a commissioner of Revenue Authority of Jonglei State;
- Sultan Chol Dau Jurkuch, a chief of the Pawiir sub-clan of the Ayual clan of Twi East County; Ajang Diing Awuol, a leader of Twi East Youth in Juba.
- Rev Canon Mark Atem Thuch, a revered senior clergy member of the Wangulei Diocese in the Episcopal Church of South Sudan (ESCSS).
- Nhial Garang Ageer, a former leader of the Red Army in Pinyudo Refugee Camp and a community leader in Kakuma Refugee Camp.
- Rev Peter Garang Deng Adi, secretary general of the ECSS' Twi East Diocese and a coordinator of Pakeer development projects.
- Kuir Dau Kuir, a former director of Norwegian People's Aid (NPA), an international NGO. Aguer Bol Kuir, a member of Twi East Youth leadership in Juba; and
- Rev Dr Isaiah Majok Dau, whose visa to attend the conference was approved but who could not travel due to other commitments.

Mamer Yak Dut, TECAA Treasurer, requests that every member pay their monthly subscription. "The Association need policies and procedures to protect operation and the people they serve. Such procedures include financial controls, an area that falls squarely into the ambit of the treasurer," Mamer said.

Galou M. M., adviser for Security and public relations. "having an outside perspective to provide non-binding strategic advice on the management of TECAA". Galou said.

This section is a summary of a conference report. It has been produced to help Twi East community members quickly understand conference information, discussions and resolutions.

The Conference discussion covered areas

SUSTAINABLE DEVELOPMENT

Diversify and strengthen Twi East's economic capacity. Develop environmentally sustainable solutions for the benefit of current and future generations.

CAPABILITY

Provide strong leadership through good governance, effective communication, and excellence in delivery.

ROAD AND CONNECTIVITY

Enhance connectivity throughout the town of Twi East and other strategic economic hubs and population centres.

IDENTITY

Sustain and grow arts and culture and preserve the importance of our social capital, which is built on heritage and history.

PLACES FOR TWI EAST PEOPLE

Create great spaces for people through innovative urban and village design.

HEALTH AND HAPPINESS

Create an environment where it is easy for people to lead safe, happy, and healthy lives.

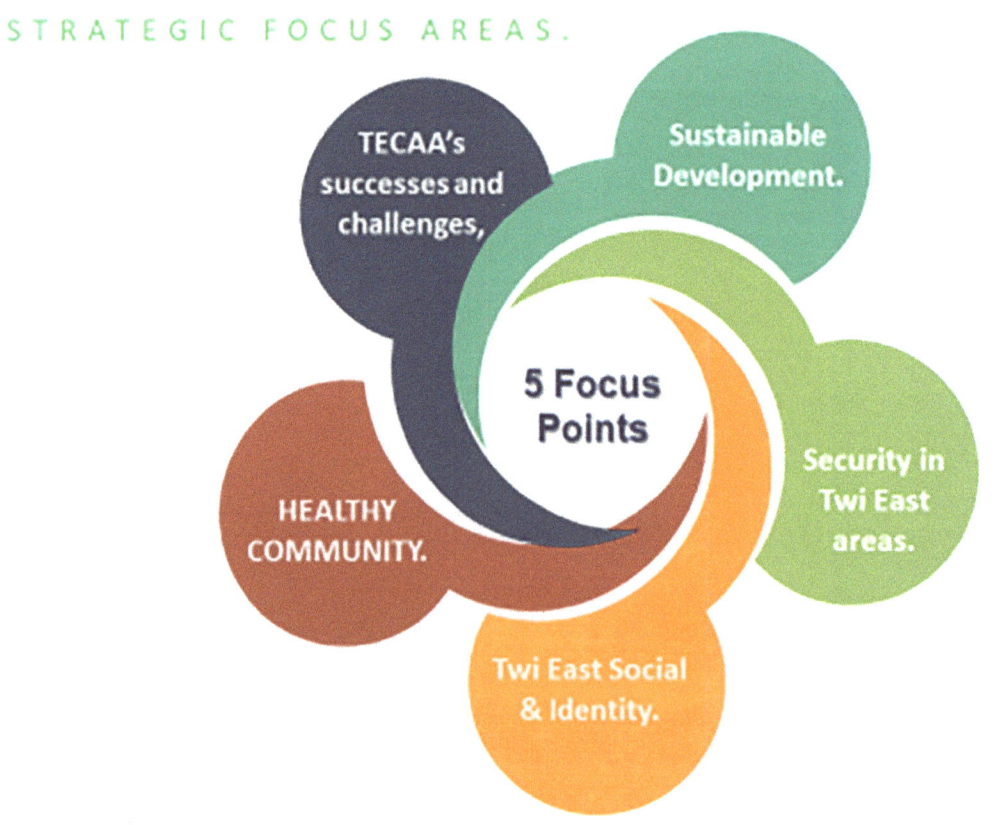

Part C: The AGM and Progress Report from the TECAA President

Deng Chol Riak, the president of TECAA, started his speech by pointing out a rather curious coincidence: that the Twi East community in the United States of America was also meeting on the day of the 2019 TECAA conference in Australia. First, he offered apologies from his wife, Adhieu Akoi Arok; Mangar Ayuel Malual, former president of TECAA; Dau Akoi Jurkuch, former commissioner of Twi East County; his Lordship Bishop Dr Isaiah Majok Dau, and many other members of TECAA who couldn't make it to the conference.

Then, the president briefly explained the prime objectives of the conference, outlining the basic modality of selecting delegates to attend the conference, including the members of the delegation who were sponsored by their families. He explained that the main purpose of having a delegation from South Sudan was to garner input from individuals with firsthand experiences of some of the challenges the conference attempted to

address. Their perspectives, he contended, would guide proposed solutions.

As part of the AGM report, the president outlined the achievements and challenges of the TECCA's Executive Committee team since it took office in December 2018.

a) Achievements
Since ascending to leadership of TECAA, the management team has achieved the following:

i. Youth empowerment: The leadership has initiated youth empowerment programs, including youth cultural activities. Some of these activities were carried out by Twi Youth leaders in the Australian Capital Territory (ACT), New South Wales (NSW), and Victoria (VIC) and included a planned 'initiation rite' for young Twi people in Melbourne on 26 October 2019. Homework programs were also planned or were underway in the cities of Toowoomba, Adelaide, and Sydney. The TECAA leadership will continue to improve on and introduce new programs for our young people.

ii. Council of Elders: The management team has established a Council of Elders, which comprises of five members from our community. Members of the Council of Elders are Benjamin Bul Duom Bul (chairperson), Adoor Akechnhial Adoor (member), Bol Kut Garang (member), Wach Duot Wach (member), and Samuel Gom Akech (member);

iii. Advisory board: The president announced a team of advisors viz.: David Dau Deng Dau (advisor for culture and development), Garang Deng Gak (advisor for legal affairs), and Golou Mayen Mabior (advisor for external affairs (special envoy));

iv. Establishment of a women's body: The leadership has promised to form a peak women's body for TECAA as soon as possible, acknowledging some difficulties in this process. Delays in formation of TECAA's women body has implications for the implementation of the Twi East Women Ambulance Project. The president reassured the community that TECAA's women's body will be formed before the end of his tenure;

v. Twi's road project: The president explained that the road project is a collective initiative in which all major Twi organizations are deeply involved. In fact, this project was initiated long before the current TECAA leadership took office. The road project is expected to address issues of insecurity by providing rapid means of movement for community protection forces. It will also provide a reliable means of delivering goods and services. There are various challenges, including funding, faced by proponents of the road project;

vi. Building harmonious relationships with sister communities of Bor and Duk: The president reported that the Twi community's relationships with its sister communities of Bor and Duk were amiable at the time his team took office and that he and his management team are working hard to improve these important relationships;

vii. Community census: The president announced that his office has carried out a census for all Twi community members in Australia. He emphasized the importance of knowing the exact numbers of Twi community members, this generating a round of applause from the floor of the conference. He presented the data per state/territory, noting that a small margin of error (±10) was possible. The total number of members of the Twi East community in Australia (as of 19 September 2019) was reported to be 5,289. This is summarized in both Table and Figure 1 below. The TECAA leadership noted some challenges while collecting the data, including lack of vital demographic attributes, such as age, gender, level of education, employment status, and clan information. It's recommended that the missing data is captured in the next census for planning purposes;

viii. Constitutional review (election rules): The president announced that his management team has formed a constitutional review subcommittee to look at election rules in the TECAA Constitution. The Constitutional Review Committee is working on the review and will forward its recommendations to the leadership team once it has completed its work. The TECAA leadership, with the help of state leadership, will share the recommendations with TECAA members in states and territories so that they can have their say before the recommendations are adopted and incorporated into the constitution. The president acknowledged that the constitution had been reviewed a few times in the recent past but stated that some sections or parts need major reworking. The members of the constitution review committee are Garang Manyang Duot (chairperson), Garang Bol Ajang (member), Lual Mayen Dhieu (member), Henry Makuei Khor (member), Jurkuch Deng Akuoch (member), Ayen Atem Chol (member), and Abul Manyuon Mayen (member).

Table 1 Presents the Twi community's population in Australia categorised by State/Territory

State/Territory	Adult Population	Under 18 Population	Total
WA	349	379	728
SA	340	432	772
VIC	530	701	1231
ACT	313	405	718
QLD	540	695	1235
NSW	193	253	446
NT	71	49	120
TAS	18	21	39
TOTAL			5,289

Figure 1 Displays the Twi community's population categorized by state/territory in a pictograph (pie chart)

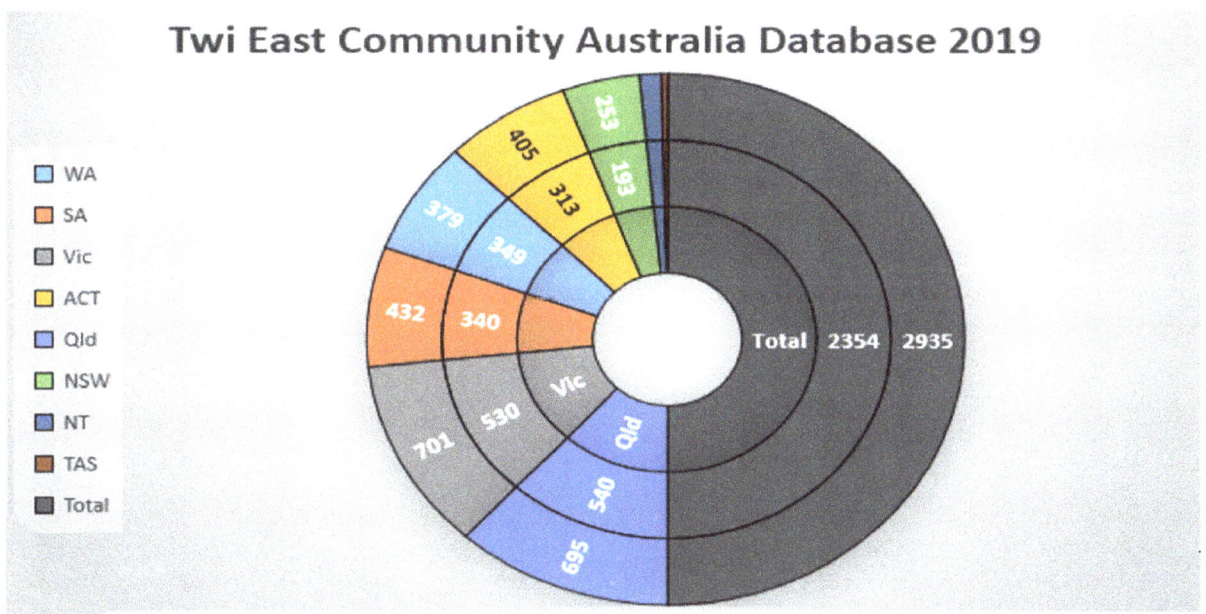

b) Challenges
The president informed the gathering that TECAA faces many organizational challenges that leaders and members should work hard to address. Some of these challenges include:

Organizational structure: There is a lack of clear structure with regard to membership fees, considering our members are also members of various Twi associations, both state and clan based. TECAA is working towards addressing this challenge to ensure efficiency.

Youth problems: Issues of youth crime are reportedly on the rise and have attracted negative publicity across Australia. The office of Twi Youth in Australia has attempted to mitigate some of these problems, and the community appreciates their selfless efforts.

Lack of unity and cooperation within the community: Our community lacks unity of purpose. TECAA is exploring options to promote unity and strengthen cooperation in areas of mutual interests, including delivery of joint community development projects at home (Twi land).

c) Appreciations
The president concluded his speech by acknowledging the efforts of state leaders and members of the TECAA management team, as named below.

State Leadership:
- Akol Dhiak Akol, chairperson (TECA VIC)
- Nuul Mayen Deng, chairperson (TECA NSW)
- Ajang Pageer Alaak, chairperson (TECA SA)
- Dau Wach Deng, chairperson (TECA QLD)
- Chut Aleer Chut, chairperson (TECA ACT)
- Majok Jawat Malek, chairperson (TECA WA)

National Leadership:
- Garang Juach Thieu, deputy president
- Ayiik Chol Anyang, secretary general
- Mamer Yaak Dut, treasurer
- Akoi Bol Nyuon, press secretary
- Lual Akoy Deng, deputy treasurer (absent with apologies)
- Majok Lual Deng, information secretary
- Garang Deng Aleu, public affairs officer
- Rev. Ayiik Chol Deng, chaplain (acting)
- Chol Akech Ajak, president of the Twi East Youth Association in Australia

d) Question & Answer Session
A question and answer session followed the president's report. Members could ask questions or make comments. A total of six questions were asked.

Question 1
Achol Garang Aguer: 'Why are women not represented in the Council of Elders, or don't we have elders who are women in our community?' She also added a supplementary question: 'Why is there no woman advisor in the advisory board?'

Answer: In answering these questions, the president acknowledged that women were not currently included in the Council of Elders or the advisory board. The president stated that he has informal advisors who are women, but he really hopes that the women's body yet to be formed will bring forth the wealth of talent our Twi women bring to our community. He emphatically asked for such oversights never to happen again.

Question 2
Dut Biar Manyuon: 'What is the leadership doing about skyrocketing dowries (bride prices) in the community'

Answer: To answer this question, the president clarified that there is no single integrated policy that regulates the amount of dowry paid by grooms and their families. Bride prices are determined by many factors, including market forces of demand and supply. The president directed the delegates to respond to this question because our community back home has engaged in exorbitant bride prices more than communities in the diaspora.

Question 3
Rev Samuel Khot Majok Tuil enquired about whether TECAA recognizes other developmental agencies and organisations, like Twi East Girls Scholarship, Jonglei Food Security, iHope, and Africa World Books Pty Ltd, that are spearheaded by members of the Twi community.

Answer: The president applauded these agencies for their dedicated services to the community, affirming that their efforts were duly recognized and appreciated. He highlighted the major activities of each organisation and congratulated the individuals behind these organizations for the incredible work they do on behalf of the community.

Question 4
Mayen Lual Arok asked whether the proposed road project is to be tarmacked (paved) or if it will be a dirt (unpaved) road.

Answer: The president stated that the kind of road that will be constructed will be dictated by the size of the budget and the availability of materials, pending the outcome of feasibility studies.

Question from Achol Garang Aguer

Question 5
Chol Achuoth Ajang enquired about the proposed Twi East women ambulance project, stating that a lack of ambulatory services contributed to a disturbing video of a sick child being carried on a stretcher on the shoulders of relatives from Wernyol to Panyagor that recently circulated on social media. Chol wondered whether our people would continue to suffer from a lack of ambulatory services since the ambulance project has been tied to the formation of a women's body.

Answer: The president appreciated Chol's question, stating that TECAA is committed to helping the community back home in any means possible. He added that this question clearly calls for good roads in Twi East. Therefore, TECAA leadership is relentlessly pursuing the proposed road project in Twi land. If there were good roads, patients could be transported (via private cars or ambulances) from anywhere in Twi East to major health centres, such as Panyagoor, in a safe and timely manner. The president implored the community to support the road project.

Question 6
Pajok Arok Duot: Pajok asked whether the government of South Sudan has formally requested communities to construct their own roads.

Answer: The president explained that community initiatives, including the proposed road project, are self-reliant initiatives and do not need government approval. A fledgling government like South Sudan's government cannot be expected to do everything, especially not during the current crisis. As a people, we are thus forced to fend for ourselves, and this was what motivated the road project, which we hope will alleviate insecurity by providing rapid means of movement for community protection forces and providing a reliable means of delivering goods and services.

e) Conclusion of the AGM Session
Bol Kut Garang, a member of the Council of Elders, gave closing remarks at the end of the AGM session. He expressed huge appreciation to the conference attendees, particularly the TECAA leaders, for organizing such a wonderful conference. He briefly spoke on the question of dowry in relation to the diaspora community. He explained that marriage is a joint venture between two families. Marriage negotiation, he said, requires frank, honest discussions between the two parties. Governor Philip Aguer Panyang is not expected to provide solutions to dowry issues. National and state governments do not legislate on private social issues, of which marriage is one. Governor Hon Philip Aguer Panyang can only advise as a member of the Twi community. In marriage negotiations, families involved need to be upfront with one another to establish a fair bride price. This can prevent young boys and girls from falling prey to alien cultures. Bol Kut then asked a rhetorical question: 'Why do our young men leave our beautiful girls in Australia and go overseas to marry?'

Furthermore, Bol Kut advised the community to staunchly uphold the rich cultures of the Twi East community. He urged members of the Twi East community to be exemplary in all that they do, just like Dr John Garang, who portrayed a good image of Twi East people to South Sudan and to the world. Bol Kut cautioned members who lack self-etiquette and acceptable mannerisms in their approaches. He strongly urged members of the Twi East community to refrain and disengage from unhealthy social media 'wars,' encouraging those who actively participate in these 'wars' in the name of 'defending a community' to instead focus on their own lives. Not everything that is said against oneself (or a community), he said, deserves a response. We should show perseverance in all circumstances, like Dr John Garang did during the liberation struggle for independence in South Sudan.

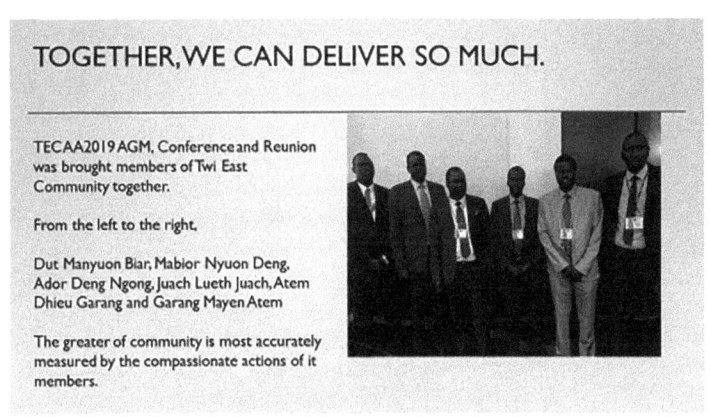

TOGETHER, WE CAN DELIVER SO MUCH.

TECAA2019 AGM, Conference and Reunion was brought members of Twi East Community together.

From the left to the right.

Dut Manyuon Biar, Mabior Nyuon Deng, Ador Deng Ngong, Juach Lueth Juach, Atem Dhieu Garang and Garang Mayen Atem

The greater of community is most accurately measured by the compassionate actions of it members.

PART D: RESEARCH AND PRESENTATION SESSION

The master of ceremonies (MC) offered the podium to David Dau Deng, TECAA's advisor on culture and community development, who took the opportunity to explain the process resulting in research papers being presented.

David thanked the presenters and researchers for offering their time and expertise and for sharing their findings with members in attendance. He went on to say that there are many experts within the Twi East community in Australia, but only a selected few were offered the opportunity to share their expertise during the 2019 TECAA conference.

David emphasized the importance of an evidence- based decision-making process, hence the reason for collating all relevant data for TECAA's future planning. He then welcomed the presenters to share their findings.

A similar conference was carried out by the previous TECAA leadership in 2017 in the city of Perth, the event bringing together members and leaders of the Twi East community from across the globe—Australia, the United States, Canada, South Sudan, and East Africa—to discuss sustainable community development, war and peace, insecurity, and more. Some wide-ranging resolutions resulted from that conference, but these are yet to be actioned.

The 2019 TECAA conference aimed to cover specific areas of concern that were not covered in the 2017 TECAA conference. These included food security through agriculture, thereby halving the number of hunger-stricken Twi people; healthcare; education; flood control; development of road access to towns and rural townships in Twi East; promotion of resettlement of displaced people in Twi East areas (it's estimated that up to two-thirds of Twi East's population live outside the county due to war-induced displacements); physical security; communication and information technology; and social amenities may attract people back to their ancestral homelands.

The present TECAA leadership understands the need to achieve sustainable socioeconomic community development that emphasises a rural-people-centred agenda. The payam associations have championed delivery services in their local communities, but there remains inequitable distribution of these services. This is where TECAA needs to step in. TECAA identified and assigned the following topics in an attempt to address the lack of services in Twi East areas:

- Sustainable development (assigned to Governor Philip Aguer Panyang);
- Technical education (assigned to uncle Mecak Ajang Alaak);
- Health and wellbeing (assigned to Daniel Garang Kuir Ayiik);
- Organisational challenges and strategies (assigned to Garang Deng Gak and David Deng Amol Dau);
- Insecurity: Challenges and opportunities (assigned to Kuer Dau Apai, no paper was submitted); Culture: Our way of life (uncle Atem Yaak Atem);
- Peace and unity (assigned to Rev Dr Isaiah Majok Dau, absent with apology).

David concluded the statement that, no organisation can success without determiner their future. This conference intent articulating aims for addressing community challenges, improvement of operation, social issues as community and association advantages.

In Conclusion

It is imperative to mention that little has been accomplished towards primary health and education and other basic services in the Twi East area since the independence of South Sudan. Barriers to access to better road, dyke constructed, education, hospitals, economic opportunities, and security in the Twi East area have led to a huge influx of members of the Twi East community to urban areas.

Photo by Galou Mabior

SUSTAINABLE DEVELOPMENT
By Hon Philip Aguer Panyang (former governor of Jonglei State)

Development may be defined as growth, improvement in people's lives, and change in our lives and welfare. But in general, development is not a one-off event. It is a process that takes time and space. Not much has developed in Twi land since the war with the North ended in 2005, but this does not mean that there have been no changes in the lives of our people. There are some people, such as police, wildlife, prison, army, and local government workers, with little income from their government employment in the organised forces, but due to inflation, most of these people cannot afford to buy even a chicken. People working in the private sector and non-governmental organisations are doing well, and so are those who have family members in the diaspora who provide remittances.

In terms of infrastructure, there has been little of note. The government is trying to maintain a few health units and centres that are faced with various challenges, as are primary education and local government administration facilities. Traditional livelihoods passed down from our ancestors continue as usual. Interventions by the diaspora in support of health services and agriculture offer bright hopes to the community and could inspire more interventions.

How Does Insecurity Affect Development?
The recent study initiated by the Jonglei State governor identified various restricting forces that affect development in the area. For example, Wernyol township has been destroyed more than three times since 1995. Markets, luaks, and huts have been burned, people have been killed, and properties have been looted and pillaged. Consequently, survivors fled from the area. Today, people are just beginning to resettle and rebuild their lives in the hope that war will come to an end.

Development is restrained by fear, war, and insecurity. The main driving forces that affect development are the political will and commitment of the government and the citizens' drive to achieve the desired change. Change happens when peace prevails, coupled with the availability of capital to engage in enterprises. Development is possible when there is a plan of what is to be done at the levels of individuals and institutions. For development to take place, there must be institutions for each field of development so that there are mechanisms for follow-up, performance monitoring and evaluation, and reporting in place.

How Does War Affect People's Confidence to Continue Building Public and Private Schools and Clinics in Twi Land?

War damages development efforts and erodes the confidence of people to continue building, raising fears of disruption. This is evident in the huge numbers of our people residing in Juba-Shirkat and the border areas who have no interest in returning home. This has greatly affected development.

The governor's report identified environmental and personal factors that may contribute to health issues. It highlighted how a lack of health facilities affects settlement of people and progress in Twi land. The answer to encouraging resettlement in the area is simple. If a member of a family falls sick and no treatment is available at home, the patient is referred to Bor or Juba or beyond and needs a supporting family member to travel with them. This often results in people abandoning their homes and has negative consequences for the village or Boma and its resident families. To resolve this problem, adequate health facilities need to be introduced to regional areas.

Secondly, a lack of diagnostic facilities and materials or equipment leads to the spread of diseases without control and treatment, reducing the overall health of the population. The population, in turn, becomes less productive, negatively affecting the economy and community in terms of social development. A lack of health facilities is linked to emigration, so in order to reduce emigration, adequate health facilities must be established.

Recommendations

The first agent of change is the human factor. To introduce change to any society, we must first teach people to embrace development. One must dream of a new world outlook, then apply that new outlook to reality to build a better life. This can be achieved through learning and changing attitudes and perceptions. Intensive community sensitisation is needed to help our people understand that they have resources and abilities that can be used to achieve development.

The correct methods and development approaches relevant to our situation must be identified in a participatory approach and utilised by the community with appropriate guidance. Other agents of change are social and economic institutions through which development can be achieved.

Long-term realistic solutions are projects that can impact the lives of our people if implemented. TECAA should select two projects to support and let each county (payam) work as a small team towards achieving the projects at a county level. For example:
- Connect Dhiam-Dhiam to the main road by constructing a 10 km road to be an all-season road. This will benefit northern parts of Jonglei as the road from Bor to Duk will take time to be constructed;
- Enable each county to support primary health centre(s), if present;
- Support John Garang Secondary School in Pakuor to become one of the best secondary schools in the region, planning for a potential transition to a tertiary education centre in the future;
- Support surveying and building of the Dhiam-Dhiam River Port;
- Support Gadiang Peace Village and Gadiang Regional Market;
- Support construction of a peace and agriculture road from Panyagoor to Gadiang and cooperate with Duk Payuel and Duk Padiet in the project of Gadiang.

The community will debate strategies on how to go about selecting any of the southern parts of the state. For instance, Penykou-Ajageer could be developed and connected to Gadiang for agriculture and resettlement. Governor Philip Aguer encouraged the community to construct a 10 km road from Dhiam- Dhiam to Piol or Maar and to connect it to Gadiang. In the future, Gadiang could become a commercial hub, with plans to connect it to Ethiopia. He encouraged people to contribute to this project, urging the community to remain united as unity is our strength.

Dhiam-Dhiam Port and the Road Project Proposal: The Concept Paper

The project proposal was designed by members of the Twi East community, and Hon Diing Akol Diing was assigned as the chairperson. Hon Dut Achuek Lual was assigned the role of deputy chairperson, and Hon Ayiei Manyok Ajak was declared a member.

Proposal Background

The project is a community-driven project along the River Nile, the largest river in Africa, which passes through several countries, including South Sudan. Jonglei State and Twi East counties are the direct beneficiaries of this great natural treasure.

During the colonial period, the former port was at Ajak-biker, north of Dhiam-Dhiam. The current port at the bank of Awai-toich of Ajak-biker used to service all southern Upper Nile colonial districts of Akobo, Bor, and Pibor. During the 1960s floods, the Ajak-biker Port was washed out, and Dhiam-Dhiam, south of Ajak-biker, became the main port in the 1980s, during SPLA/M's liberation war.

The Dhiam-Dhiam Port is on the Awan-baai bank of the White Nile River. It is common knowledge to all local communities that the Dhiam-Dhiam Port was the only outlet and inlet for ferrying SPLA soldiers, recruits, and logistics to and from the west bank of the White Nile River during the war. It was also the only port through which United Nations agencies could deliver humanitarian assistance or relief rations to populations in Twi East, Bor, and Duk.

Justification of the Dhiam-Dhiam Port and the Connecting 10 km Road

If a port and a 10 km road running from Dhiam-Dhiam Port to Alelei Cattle Camp's road junction on the Juba-Malakal road are built, both the port and the road linking the port to the Juba-Malakal road will create lifeline access to the people of Twi East counties, Duk counties, northern Bor counties, and neighbouring states of Biech, Akobo, and Boma.

This construction will, most importantly, create remarkable economic opportunities that will stimulate business activities and create wealth and job opportunities that could transform people's lives and spur economic development at local and state levels. The road from Dhiam-Dhiam Port to Alelei Camp on the Juba-Malakal road will be:

- 2 km from Dhiam-Dhiam Port to Getwer, which is rather low and can become sodden and swampy during the rainy season;
- 2 km from Getwer to an uncompleted dyke constructed by the former Jonglei Canal Project in 1983;
- 2 km from Patiou to the junction on the Juba-Malakal road, which is dry but can become sodden and swampy during the rainy season.

In summary, the 6 km from Getwer Cattle Camp to the existing completed dyke at Patiou run in a lowland, which is prone to being sodden and swampy during the rainy season but is mostly dry in the summer months from January to March/April.

Expected Advantages or Benefits of the Dyke and Road

- The completion of the 1983 Jonglei Canal Project dyke that runs from the west of Jalle to the northernmost tip of Twi East County will prevent floods from entering inhabited areas of northern Bor counties, Twi East counties, and neighbouring communities. It will create an access point and a mode of transport to and from the Dhiam-Dhiam Port, thus creating business activities on the port, in adjacent areas, and beyond;
- The completion of the 1983 Jonglei Canal Project dyke will lessen the cost of construction of a road from Patiou to Dhiam-Dhiam;
- The new dyke will create investment opportunities for international businesses, thus creating employment opportunities for locals, spurring growth and income, and improving local gross domestic product (GDP);
- Completion of the 1983 Jonglei Canal Project dyke will cost less in terms of finances and material than constructing a new dyke;
- The land that will be reclaimed by the dyke construction can be used for agricultural purposes, including crop farming and animal husbandry;
- If a new (back-up) dyke is constructed to the west of the 1983 Jonglei Canal dyke, it will reinforce the main dyke and force backflow to the White Nile River, minimizing chances of floods.

Expected Disadvantages
- If the new road is not well constructed, it will be more dangerous to people and animals in the area. The high speed of the water could lead to flooding of inhabited areas;
- It will be very expensive to construct the road due to the lowliness of the land. The area is too swampy and wet, so modern machinery will be needed in order to build a flying bridge, and this construction will be expensive and labour-intensive;
- Constructing a new road from Patiou to Dhiam-Dhiam will be time consuming;
- The new road will need a wider space and higher level, and it will also need to be stronger in order to avoid water overflow. The dyke in the east will need wider space, and this will lead to soil erosion
- as the land around the dyke is washed away by water;
- If the direct road constructed from Patiou to Dhiam-Dhiam is high and thick, it will always block
- water's passage, and that will result in either overflowing or breaking of the dyke.

Continuation of Jonglei Canal Dyke

Twi East populations are being threatened by insecurity from Murle in the east and chronic flooding from the west. Communities are pushing for the continuation of the old dyke, where Jonglei Canal dyke stopped, so that they can reclaim the land. The communities and stakeholders are bound to the port, road, and dyke initiatives for socio-economic development and resettlement of displaced populations.

The community has shown serious commitment to the project during consultations, and we believe that all stakeholders—Jonglei State Government and national government investors—will have to commit to supporting it technically and financially.

By constructing a port and 10 km road from Dhiam-Dhiam to Alelei Cattle Camp road junction on the Juba- to-Malakal main road, a lifeline access point will be provided to people of Twi East, Duk, and Bor South counties and neighbouring states of Biech, Akobo, and Boma.

Hon Panyang discussed the issue of insecurity in the area of Twi East as a threat to everyone in the state. When there is calm and stability in a location, people say that there is security. Insecurity in the Twi East area is caused by politically motivated insurgency affecting the whole of South Sudan; by cattle raiding from Boma, Bieh, or Fangak; and by child abduction from Boma.

Factors that need to change or be introduced for insecurity to be resolved:
- National peace
- Local peace agreements with neighbours
- Recruitment and training of a professional and effective police force in Twi East and in neighbouring states and counties
- Disarmament of armed civilians in our state and in all neighboring states
- Court punishment of criminals and establishment of prisons to house and rehabilitate the convicted

Challenges to security at home:
- Lack of trained and well-equipped police o Scattered settlements
- Lack of roads
- Insufficient means of communication
- Lack of prisons

Solutions to insecurity in Twi East:
- Recruit and train police
- Declare war against criminality
- Provide a Motorola system of communication to all Boma and connect them with bases and power for charging in all the payams
- Support the idea of Gadiang Peace Village and connect it to Boma and Aja-ageer

Why Returning to TWI Land is Rational and Feasible

By Hon Atem Yaak Atem
(Formerly Deputy Minister of Information in the government of South Sudan, an elder and intellectual)

South Sudan is one of the richest places on Earth. Its wealth consists of vast arable land; generous rainfall for more than half of the year; rich flora and fauna; and good, patient people. That is the positive side of the story. The negative side is that we are among the world's poorest people. Why? This essay is an attempt to look at some of the factors behind the problems, most of them of our own making. These are twofold: the city and our mindset. Our mindset convinces most of us that living in the city is bliss, that government jobs are the dream of nearly every schoolchild in our country since formal education was introduced.

Cities and Their Attractions

Centres that later evolved into cities in Europe and the Middle East—Rome, Athens, Jericho, Uruk, Carthage—began as settlements for a few inhabitants, who over time began to organise themselves into communities whose members specialised in industry, governance, and intellectual and spiritual pursuits. As the city dwellers lived near sparsely inhabited virgin lands, they derived their food from country. Over time, influxes into the cities increased, especially after the Industrial Revolution in Europe. More often than not, these cities were capitals of their countries, and that meant that they housed governments and their branches, namely the executive, legislative, and judiciary branches.

Capital cities were often the headquarters of religious organisations, centres of learning, and research facilities. Industry and manufacturing grew. In later centuries, amenities, such as electricity, piped water, health care facilities, transport, and higher education, were introduced to satisfy the urban populations, making the cities coveted destinations for rural migrants. The result was that cities swelled, sometimes beyond their carrying capacity. That is why today, megacities like Cairo (over 20 million citizens) and Lagos (about 17 million citizens) have double the entire population of South Sudan.

Attitudes Towards Rural Dwellers

The relationship between cities and rural areas consisted of two factors: production and consumption. The rustics acted as the producers, while the denizens acted as the consumers. Instead of considering the two sets of communities as mutually beneficial and reinforcing, unfortunately, city dwellers tended to show a condescending attitude towards rural populations. 'Rustics' originally referred to country people, but over time, the word has become abusive; some people use it to refer to a person who is uncouth, uncivilised, or lacking in social skills.

In our own society, we have jal pac, a Shilluk word that is a synonym of the terms stated above. Until recent years, it was not uncommon to hear the word 'natives' being used by urban, English-literate Southern Sudanese people to describe their compatriots living in rural South Sudan or illiterate urban dwellers. Having borrowed the terms from foreign rulers, namely the British, abusers of the words forgot that they were also natives of Sudan, regardless of how much book learning they had acquired.

Problems of Congestion in Cities

With the populations of urban centres increasing exponentially, available services have struggled to keep up, leading problems such as unemployment, poverty, and service shortages in health, housing, and education to arise. In such an environment, crime rates are bound to increase. I do not need to go far to provide examples. The following stories explain the situation I witnessed in Juba when I was there for four months in 2013.

Sedentary Games Under Trees

In 2013, I found myself jobless and decided to employ myself. There was no better entry into the job market than to work as a newspaper owner. The first step in that direction was to hire a modest three-bedroom building in the Thong-piny area, not far from Victoria Hotel, which was near some foreign missions and a ministerial complex.

Each morning as I went to work, seven days a week, I passed through a residential neighbourhood with giant, shady trees. Under those tropical trees, I saw a group of young Dinka men sitting in the shade, most of them bent over something on the ground. They were there from eight in the morning until bedtime. What were they doing there? I became curious about their daily business. On the third day I saw them, I decided to test my curiosity. I moved very close to them. The young men, I discovered, were playing Tök ku Rou, a game of numbers using holes in the ground, popular in rural Dinka communities, especially during the dry season when there is little work on family farms. I left soon afterwards, going to mind my own business.

I soon learned from some of the participants that at mealtimes—lunch and dinner—they reported to the homes, where they lived mostly with their relatives, most of whom worked for the government. When I asked one of the youths, he told me that some of them were primary school dropouts, while others had obtained secondary school leaving certificates. They all complained of unemployment, meaning a lack of government jobs, specifically office work.

Handwashing Launderers

A few steps from where I worked, a group of Ugandans, men and women, in their thirties and forties rented a cheap three-room house. Their life was communal. One room was for women, the second for men. They led a simple life, sharing matoke, their national dish of boiled green bananas, and sometimes Sudanese asida. One of them told me that they rarely ate meat, which they considered a luxury. All of them slept either on mattresses or mats, which were spread out on the floor.

Though I was not interested in the lifestyle these neighbours led, how they spent their money said a lot about the purpose of their stay in South Sudan. The third room in the building was set aside for commercial laundry, the core business they ran. As was to be expected, their customers were all South Sudanese people. Since the Ugandans did not own a washing machine—machines were expensive, and there was only an erratic supply of electricity in Juba—they washed manually, using water they bought in huge plastic barrels from Eritrean truck drivers. For pressing the clothes, they washed, they bought sacks of charcoal to power their iron boxes.

One would conclude that a business with such overhead costs would yield very little by way of profit to the people operating it. But from the interviews I conducted with some of them, the Ugandans were not losing money. I was told that washing and ironing a shirt and a pair of trousers cost a customer 3 South Sudanese pounds, which was quite a lot of money (at the time, 1 US dollar was equal to 2.5 pounds at the bank). I learned that each of the launderers earned an average of 120 pounds a day, and as they all shared accommodation and meals, daily expenditure per a person was under 5 pounds, so they saved the rest, which they regularly sent home in dollars.

Determination and Thrift

The laundry workers' story reminded me of a Kenyan grandmother who once worked as a labourer in one of the hotels in Juba. The lady, probably in her sixties, who declined my interview, was said to have built a permanent house in her native Central Province with the money she made working in South Sudan, where she did chores such as pushing wheelbarrow, carrying the rubbish from the hotel, and even assisting construction workers to build a hotel extension. The house she built might have been modest, but it was proof of her determination and ability to improve her life and the lives of her family with the proceeds of her labour, old as she was. Venturing to South Sudan offered her an opportunity to make money that would have been almost impossible in her native home.

To me, the woman's story and that of the Ugandan laundry people were truly newsworthy. Although it is public knowledge that there are thousands of non-South Sudanese nationals making a living in the country—among them, the truck drivers selling raw water from the Nile, the operators of refrigerated vans ferrying fresh fish every morning from Terekeka to Juba for sale to hotels and restaurants, street cleaners, and vendors of imported vegetables and eggs—I found the story of the Ugandan laundry workers enlightening. They were making handsome returns from their trades.

A Word of Caution
Before I proceed to the next narratives, I must make it clear that by citing the cases of non-South Sudanese nationals working and making money in Juba in areas neglected by the locals, I am in no way supporting xenophobic sentiments against people from neighbouring countries. To do that would not only be irresponsible; it would be dangerous. We have seen the negative results of anti-foreigner expressions and actions in other parts of Africa. South Sudanese people need to be tolerant and observe the rule of law.

The reason I am compelled to recount success stories of people from South Sudan's neighbouring countries is to help my fellow South Sudanese people learn the value of hard work and modesty. Many South Sudanese people, especially young people, must change their attitudes and perceptions of the true meanings of employment and unemployment. If we are at all looking for a scapegoat in our sorry situation, we do not have look far; the culprit is us and our mindset, which has resulted in induced laziness and the accompanying desire to harvest where we have not sown our own seeds.

We should be vigilant against irresponsible sentiments that would consider fellow Africans who have come to South Sudan to make a living as people who have come to rob us of our jobs. A close look at the factors behind our socioeconomic difficulties will reveal that most of our problems are self-inflicted. The influx of foreigners into our country is not the cause of our poverty. It could be a symptom of our inability to help ourselves with the opportunities and resources at our disposal. The presence and success of foreigners and their businesses should act an inspiration to us. We can learn how to manage small businesses from them and work to become profitable.

South Sudanese people should avoid what has happened in post-apartheid South Africa, where some citizens have vented their anger and frustration over unemployment and rising crime on fellow Africans who have gone there to make a living.
South Sudan with its abundant natural resources—water; huge, untapped arable land, and proud, resilient people—can offer opportunities to its citizens and to others, especially our brothers and sisters who stood with us during the bitter liberation struggle. They gave us much needed support when we had nothing to give in return. We cannot forget them now or blame them for our ills, nearly all of which arise as a result of our own folly.

But blaming ourselves perpetually is not going to help us. We should instead encourage fellow citizens who show initiative that can help to change our collective mindset. We as a society need to question the notions that hold people back from improving their lives. One of these is the perception of employment. The following stories illustrate a direction for our young people, policy makers, parents, and schoolteachers.

A Shoeshine Schoolboy
Modi was about 15 years old and attended a Juba primary school. I came to know him when he approached me as I was about to enter the compound, I worked in. Schools had closed for the day, and Modi wanted to shine my shoes. Though the leather shoes I was wearing were not in need of brushing, I allowed him to clean them. I thought what he was doing was more honourable than begging and wanted to help him.

As he brushed, he began to chat. He informed me that he was staying with his family, consisting of his parents and four siblings. His father worked with the government and earned modest pay, but it wasn't enough to support the family. Modi's earnings from his shoe shining job, which he did after school and over the weekends, helped him buy what he needed. When he made enough money, he gave part of it to his family, he said. I told him what he was doing was good and that he should continue to do it.

To encourage Modi further, I told him that a former American president, Lyndon B. Johnson, had also cleaned shoes to earn pocket money as a student. Modi gave a smile of approval and pride. As we were leaving, I advised him that he should pay more attention to his lessons. He thanked me and went to look for more customers.

Seller of Toiletries

Deng, a young Dinka man from Aweil, came to my office. I assumed that he was looking for a job. He was not. He made that point immediately. He was a roving seller and had come to sell some of his wares to me. They consisted of middle-grade perfumes, combs, handkerchiefs, and nail clippers.

Deng was a persuasive salesperson, using just the right amount of humour; these were tools of the trade he had learned in Khartoum during the war. Deng was fluent in Dinka and spoke good colloquial Arabic. He also had some working knowledge of English. While we were talking, he moved from one medium to the next, holding the listener captive. He was very good at communicating. When I joked with him that girls, mainly those from the Dinka ethnic group, would not accept him as a husband given that petty traders were not well regarded, Deng quickly interrupted me: 'Even when they [the petty traders] have bags full of money?'

I could not resist laughing, and neither could my colleagues, who were listening to our conversation. Although I had stopped wearing perfume a long time ago, I bought a bottle, which I later gave to a friend, who cherished it.

Mindsets About Jobs Among South Sudanese People

The act of pinning down the mindset of a group of people belongs to the social psychology discipline. For our purpose here, we do not need to get into the reasons why a fairly high number of South Sudanese people, particularly those with formal education, tend to despise certain occupations regardless of the earnings they offer. However, it could be guessed that part of our attitude towards jobs is influenced by the fact that many South Sudanese young people dream of becoming ministers, ambassadors, MPs, and doctors. They frequently strive to hold high-profile positions that offer opportunities to be in the news and to be positively spoken about in social circles. The words 'office' and 'officials' read and sound like magic bullets, even when the holders of such positions are far from decision making and are offered little pay. The title gives satisfaction in and of itself.

'Role Models' of a Kind

It is said that people who have been marginalised and oppressed a great deal and for too long tend to covet the ways and the style of their oppressors. South Sudanese people, especially members of the intelligentsia, were denied positions of power and prestige before and after the independence of Sudan from the joint British-Egyptian rule in 1956.

It is not surprising that Ismail el Azhari, Ibrahim Abboud, Mohammed Ahmed Mahjoub, Sadiq el Mahdi, and Jaafar Nimeiri, to name some of the Northern political and military leaders, exercised power in public spaces, flanked by motorcade, blaring sirens, and awe.

Does it come as a surprise to anyone that a speaker of parliament, even a city mayor, might be escorted by a motorcade like a head of state? Status symbols are everywhere in our cities. Many systems, processes, and privileges are not there for the personal protection and safety of the functionary. They are instead designed to impress onlookers in shows of power, status, and self-importance.

This also applies to jobs, with white-collar jobs serving as the pinnacle many young people aspire towards. Blue collar or menial jobs, even when they are highly rewarded, are perceived as undesirable by many young people entering the employment market.

As dream jobs are mostly found in the national, state, and sometimes county capitals, the rush of unemployed youths to urban centres continues to expand cities. Cities also have other attractions, including clean drinking water and electricity, the latter increasingly a necessity in the era of technology. Most of us who were born and grew up in rural areas think that living in a city with access to all its amenities is the best thing since the discovery of penicillin.

Public Servants Are Indispensable to the Life of a State

It would be unfair to condemn cities and those who live in them. That cities become overcrowded has never been the aim of their founders; it is what they offer, by way of jobs and amenities, that draws people in. Originally, towns began as centres where the business of governing the people was located.

A country or a state is like a business concern. It requires managers to run it in the interest of its citizens. These people are the civil servants who plan and carry out the day to day affairs of the country. At the apex of the state is the executive in the form of the cabinet, then the legislature and the judiciary, each with specific roles to perform for the viability of the state. The personnel operating those institutions, whether their performance is satisfactory or otherwise, is not the point; public servants are indispensable.

From a teleological point of view, these public servants (among them, the non-political civil servants) should be seen as volunteers, despite the rewards they receive in forms of salaries and emoluments. Their services are poorly rewarded in comparison with managers of multinational corporations, whose yearly incomes often surpass millions of dollars. In fact, the monthly salary of a government minister in some African countries is less than what a manual worker gets each month in Australia.

Beyond those employed by the state as producers of knowledge, health care workers and specialists, and those working in the private sector in industries like manufacturing, the other group of people whose stay in cities can be justified are the families and children of these workers. Logically speaking, those who do not belong to the categories listed have no business staying in cities; they should go the countryside to breed livestock, catch fish, and till the land to grow food for themselves, with surplus allotted for sale to urban dwellers.

Why the Rural Area is the Right Place to Be?

In 2004, a local Australian church, which was attended by several members of my family, asked my wife and I to talk about the difficulties families faced during the war in Sudan, which was then ongoing. My wife told a story that moved the congregation almost to tears. She narrated the flight of Sudanese refugees from Itang to Southern Sudan. With three very young children, including a three-month-old daughter, she travelled with many of the refugees heading towards Nasir, braving heavy rains, mosquitos, hunger, and exhaustion. Children were carried on their parents' backs or shoulders.

I told a different story. Although I thanked the Australian authorities for accepting my family to settle in Australia, where my children were attending school, I told the congregation that I had no convincing reason for being in Australia. I had to explain why my role in the adopted home was almost irrelevant.

Australia, I told them that the Australian society was an ordered one, and that there was nothing that I could do to improve it. The country and its level of progress was a challenge not only to me as an individual but also to other migrants from places where poverty and conflict are common.

The explanation I gave then would in years to come be confirmed by a Nigerian in England. Writing a letter to the editor in the November 2017 issue of British monthly magazine History Today, Adesanya Adewusi said, 'Nigeria, where I was born, should be more prosperous than the UK given its resources. However, the system is so broken that people can no longer rely on the government to carry out its obligation. Until mindsets change, Africa will remain the world's poorest continent.'

Almost to the disbelief of my audience, my understanding of the disparity between Australia and the soon- to-be independent South Sudan had something to do with what people do. I did not claim that I alone had the power to turn South Sudan into a prosperous country. However, my part to play was and is to participate in public education via mass media. It was a given by the media scholars of our youth that in preliterate societies like that of South Sudan, radio was an ideal medium for mass mobilisation and enlightenment, working as one of the most effective tools of social transformation. As a journalist, I told the congregation, my presence in Africa was more important than in Australia, even when I was teaching at the University of Newcastle and later at TAFE (Technical and Further Education) in Granville, Sydney.

Why I Want to Return to the Land
Since entering secondary school, I have lived in cities, in Sudan, in Europe, in West Africa, and today in Australia. Though I cannot deny the benefits of living in cities, which offer a high level of health care, academic, media, and public facilities, I have had enough of city living. The downsides of cities include pollution of all kinds, ranging from noise to fumes from vehicles, and the prevalence of unhealthy food, including those using preservatives and hormones. Many cities are developed and are taken good care of by local councils and relevant government departments. Thus, they do not need my contribution. Conversely, the countryside in my native South Sudan is crying out for what people like me can give.

A Move to the Countryside Thwarted by War
In 2012, I sent a lorry loaded with poles of teak and bamboo to the town of my birth in Pakuoor Village in the Kongor area in what was previously known as Twi East. My plan was to use the materials for a house and shelter for livestock—cattle, sheep, and goats. After structures were set up, including solar panels on the roof of the house I was going to live in, I moved in and settled in the area, where I was going to engage in agriculture and animal husbandry. Then, the war broke out in 2013.

The Resources Available and the Education and Knowledge Required to Capitalize on Them

By Mecak Ajang Alaak

Brief biographical note of Mecak Ajang Alaak, was born in 1944 in South Sudan and educated in Rumbek Secondary School. He was the foundation director of the refugee schools in Ethiopia and Kakuma Refugee Camp in Kenya where the refugee children known as "Lost Boys and Girls" were. At the younger age of 20 years Ajang was a wrestling champion of Ayoor of Kongor Wundit (1964-1966). He was the record holder in high jump in the Africa School Athletic Competition (Jumped 1.85 meters high) in Addis Ababa 1967. Mr Ajang has a degree in mathematics and physics from the University of Liberia, West Africa. He also studied French at Lubumbashi University in the Democratic Republic of the Congo DRC. He has advance diploma from the University of Leeds UK in education management. He has also worked with ministry of Education in the Sudan for many years. He taught mathematics and Physics in Rumbek Secondary School and Malek Senior Secondary School as the first headmaster in Jonglei Province. Before he left Sudan in 1988, he was the Director for Educational Planning, Development and Scholarships for South Sudan. In Australia Ajang was a member of the Board of Director of the Australian Refugee Association, South Australia. He was also the former lay member of Anglican Church Synod of South Australia (1998-2005).

Importance Of Technical Education

The aim of this presentation is to educate the community about the natural resources we have and the ways in which we can teach young people to use these to achieve development goals.

In my presentation, I will cover:
- Geography of the Twi area
- People of the Twi East community
- Population changes in the Twi area
- Peace and reconciliation in the country
- Natural resources available
- Technical education needed for our youth for development goals
- The way forward

Geography of the Twi Area

The Twi area is located in Jonglei State of the Upper Nile region in South Sudan, east of the River Nile. The Nile River and the network of small rivers meander through marshland, swamps, and lakes and discharge water into the great wetland of the Sudd. According to research done in the area, as much as half of the inflowing water is lost to evaporation. It was due to this loss of water that the Jonglei Canal was planned to pass through Twi area, directing the water to the junction of the River Nile and River Sobat, south of Malakal.

The Jonglei Canal is not under discussion here. I would advise intellectuals from the area to read and study the Jonglei Canal's advantages and disadvantages for the community.

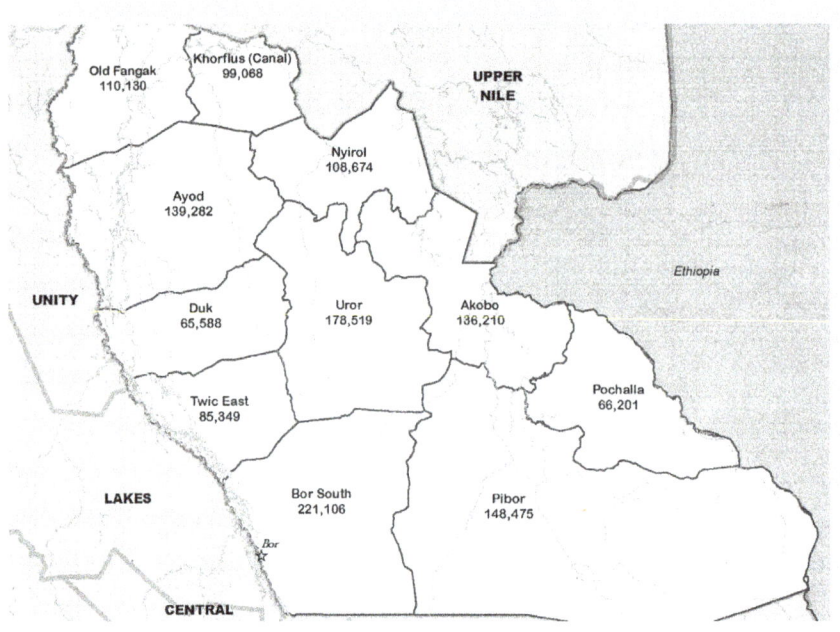

Map of Twi East within Jonglei State
Total area size: 5,936 square km
Population density: 19.88 per square km
Source: Jonglei State

The Twi people are between Nyarweng of Duk County and Athoc of Bor South County. Twi people are divided into five sections: Lith, Kongor, Nyuak, Ajuong, and Pakeer. These sections are further divided into smaller lineage segmentation groups known as Wut in Dinka. Wut refers to the smallest formal territorial unit of the tribe; the plural of Wut is Wuor.

The following diagram shows the five main sections of Twi and their Wuor.

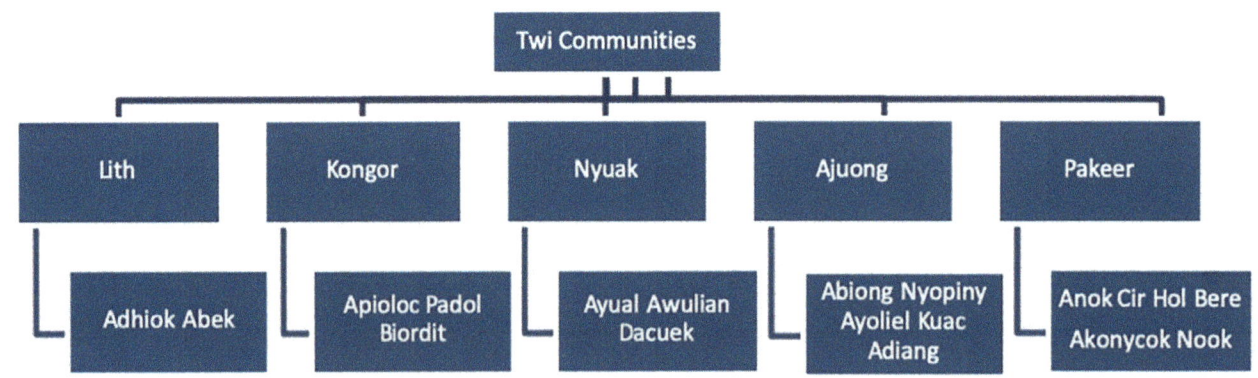

This diagram is for small children who were born in the diaspora.

The Twi population changes as a result of wars in the country. The following population censuses—the 1983 population census, the 2008 population census, and the 2012 local population census—are provided to show the changes that have taken place.

	Payam	1983 Census	2008 Census	2012 Local Census
1	Lith	13,693	10,712	21,345
2	Kongor	21,673	22,180	26,207
3	Nyuak	33,120	21,121	38,849
4	Ajuong	8,422	14,760	17,913
5	Pakeer	14,340	16,576	22,616
Total		91,248	85,349	126,930

	Payam	2008 Census	2012 Local Census	Population Increase	Population Increase (%)
1	Lith	10,712	21,345	10,633	33.2%
2	Kongor	22,180	26,207	4,027	8.3%
3	Nyuak	21,121	38,849	17,728	31.3%
4	Ajuong	14,760	17,913	3,153	9.7%
5	Pakeer	16,576	22,616	6,040	15.4%
Total		85,349	126,930	41,581	19.6%

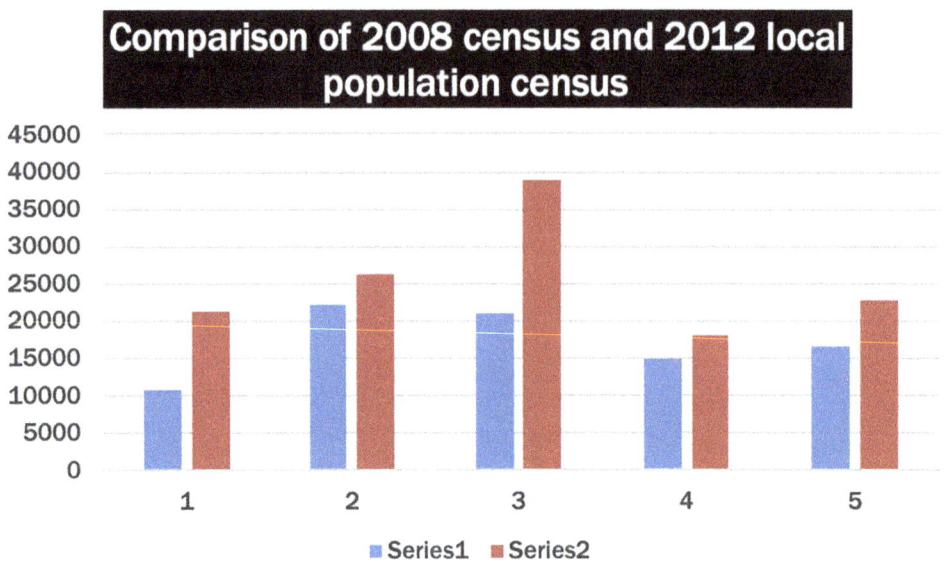

Column1 (in red) refers to the 2012 local census.

The 2012 local census was conducted by the chiefs. They registered their people, including those who were not at home. Our challenge here as the people of Twi community is the next census. In chapter one, article 1.2.14 of the Revitalized Agreement on the Resolution of the Conflict in the Republic of South Sudan (R- ARCSS), it is stated that the Revitalized Transitional Government of National Unity will conduct a national population census before the end of the transitional period.

The period of this transitional government will only be three years, and our people will still be in displacement camps and refugee camps in neighboring countries. How can we make the Twi area attractive enough to encourage our people to return home before the population census?

In order to develop our country and utilize our natural resources, we must have peace. Where there is friction, no work is done. We must work for peace in the following three areas:

I will not talk about peace as it is not the focus of this talk. What I will do is attach the paper I wrote about the reconciliation between Ayual and Dacuek, dated 8 May 2011.

The following natural resources are available in our community, but we remain poor because wars and a lack of technical knowledge have resulted in them not being utilised.

- Good agricultural land
- Water resources (Sudd system)
- Forest resources (Thau, adok, timber, and others)
- Wildlife and tourism
- Fish and fisheries
- River transport and river ports (Dhiam-Dhiam)
- Livestock (cows, sheep, and goats)
- Soil, sand, and grass
- Solar energy
- Oil and gas

We need technical education in industrial, practical, and mechanical arts and applied sciences to equip our youth to achieve development goals. My presentation of today is aimed at all the South Sudanese people in Australia, in the diaspora, and back home in South Sudan and Africa. With the training of our people in technology, science, and engineering, the resources we have in our country can be developed quickly. We must use what we have to get what we want.

Some of our South Sudanese youth here in the diaspora and at home have done well in their studies, but achievements have been predominantly in the arts. Of South Sudanese people who have finished their university education in Australia, few of people are working in their fields of study. The rest who are physically fit are working manual jobs.

Most of our children do not take up technical subjects or go to trade schools because their parents and the community do not encourage them to do so. Reasons for this include:
- The community and parents discourage young people from taking technical subjects because they don't result in degrees;
- The children's basic knowledge about literacy and numeracy skills are low at primary level;
- At secondary level, our children struggle with mathematics and sciences;
- Many children complete secondary school without a clear plan about their future careers and the courses they should take at university level.

Recommendations

The way forward in encouraging our youth to take up technical subjects is for parents and the community to:
- Learn about the importance of technical education.
- Support children in primary school to develop good literacy and numeracy skills;
- Support children in secondary school to develop good mathematics and science skills;
- Establish good links with the schools where children are studying;
- Help children in secondary schools to identify and pursue good career choices in technical subject areas;
- Support secondary school students to get holiday jobs in technical fields;
- Form committees in each of the Australian states to support young people in their studies of technical subjects;
- Coordinate the work of the state communities with assistance from state leadership;
- Support young relatives in Africa to study technical subjects with incentives, financial or otherwise; o Encourage the government of South Sudan to establish technical education institutions.

Conflict Management

By Mecak Ajang Alaak, Twi East Elder/Intellectual

The letter was address to Nyuak Community Intellectuals, Chiefs, Church leaders, and Elders on 8 May 2012. The letter about Peace, Reconciliations and the Co-existence of Nyuak Community in Twi East County.

First and foremost, I would like to express my gratefulness to Twi East County intellectuals, chiefs and elders for their tireless work trying to address issues that have largely affected the citizens, and sharply split the Twi East County. I am honored by the Twi East county leadership and their passionate efforts that have set forth a viable framework to bring peace and reconciliations between Dacuek and Ayual communities.

I have witnessed the current destructive nature of the conflicts in the area which have devastated the whole country. Concurrently, I was going home to attend the funeral rite of my elder sister who was killed with six members of her family by cattle raiders. She was about eighty years old. My journey home has allowed me to explore the aftermath of the conflict in the county. We cannot afford to sit idly and think that this problem will disappear on its own. It is time to act and provide strategic plans that would address the conflict peacefully. The last conflict that erupted at a disputed church location has claimed many lives. I am concerned about the magnitude and extent this conflict has reached. The outbreak and spread of this conflict to different cities in South Sudan and Kenya is escalating. Young people from both sides must be stopped and educated about consequences of conflicts. I am certainly aware that there is nothing to be won in this fighting because both communities are losing in all possible directions. We are inextricably tied by one destiny. Any community could engage in fighting, but their strength lies in their reconciliation, peace and coexistence. It is important to put our differences behind for the sake of humanity and for our common values.

The Nyuak community elders, intellectuals and church leaders must step forward to take lead, especially individuals from Dacuek, Ayual and Awulian. So that unity and reconciliation are restored. The classical example on how to resolve conflict was first done by Alaak Gong Kuol. He singles handedly stopped fighting between Dacuek and Kongor. This spiritual leader took matters into his own hands, and asked Kongor and Dacuek to unite and fight common enemy. These two groups (Kongor-Dacuek) immediately joined their hands to fight against the external invaders. It is very important to learn from past experienced leaders in order to peacefully solve our current issues. The main aim is to bring peace, unity and reconciliations (PUR) in Twi East which can be replicated across South Sudan. PUR stands for Peace, Unity and Reconciliations in Dinka, and in English it means hoe which is simply a tool for weeding out unwanted grass.

I am sorry to see these two communities fighting at a time of independence. Because of the continuation of revenge, the area has been deserted. The families are feeling insecure, the houses that were being built have ceased. The construction of schools, and the gardening stopped. Furthermore, Sudani-networks at Duk de Chut near Wangulei–Nyuak Payam has ceased to serve the community. The little progressive development that was happening in Twi East County is diminishing. The rainy season has already started. As we speak, people are not preparing their gardens for cultivation because they fear for possible attacks. It is an embarrassment to have professional SPLA soldiers engage in keeping peace in the inter-community conflict. The work of the professional soldiers is to protect our national territorial integrity which is the boundary of South Sudan. We, the members of these communities should provide a viable resolution to this conflict.

The following circumstances have been deemed as obstacles to Peace Unity and Reconciliation in Twi East County.

- The request for the removal or resignation of the Twi East commissioner: The removal of the commissioner is not the responsibility of Twi East citizens. The power to remove the commissioner is enshrined at prerogative of the executive of Jonglei State.
- The request for the appeal to be done immediately: The question of the appeal is at the judicial discretions to decide when the appropriation judicial decision is deliberated.
- The removal of the Juba-Twi East Community Mr Presidentperson: The removal of the Mr Presidentman cannot be demanded by Nyuak Community alone but with the consent of the Twi Community in Juba.

The conflict between these communities should be resolved by all Twi community members and spearheaded by intellectuals. The intellectuals on both sides should take the lead in bringing peace and reconciliation between the two groups. However, hardliners from both sides must stop and change direction for betterment of our community. This will also make it easy to govern and stabilize Twi County. Efforts to bring peace and reconciliation to these two communities should be supported and encouraged by all people, including diverse groups from three counties of Bor, Duk and Twi East. We should not dwell on the causes of the conflict; however, the intellectuals, chiefs and church must work together to neutralize the situation. Anything beyond our control must be left to judges.

We are part of the genesis of this liberation's struggles that have given freedom and justice to millions of South Sudanese and the marginalized areas. It is shamefully and directly hurting our image to see people sacrificing their lives for the freedom of others. Instead of happily celebrating the independence of the Republic of South Sudan, they awfully turned around to kill themselves. It is our responsibility to solve this conflict and put forth foundations to resolve future conflicts. We must remember those who fought for liberty, instead of eliminating our brothers. I challenge all of you to reconcile, restore peaceful coexistence in Twi East County, in Jonglei and among South Sudanese communities in general.

Setting a Foundation for a Healthy Community

by Daniel Garang

Author biography: Daniel Garang Kuir is a member of the Twi East Community Association of Australia. He is a senior medical scientist, holding a master's degree in medical science and a bachelor's degree in biomedicine. He is a former Jesuit Refugee Service (JRS) and Australian Commonwealth scholar and has extensive experience and training in medical pathology. He has been working in the field of medical pathology for the past 14 years. As a senior medical scientist, Garang oversees the operation of a diagnostic medical microbiology laboratory of the Specialist Diagnostic Services Pathology at Footscray Hospital. He has published peer-reviewed work in medical journals in Australia. He has also attended and presented some of his work in various professional forums in Australia. Garang is a member of the Australian Society of Microbiology. His areas of interest are antimicrobial resistance and antimicrobial susceptibility testing, medical microbiology and immunology, medical parasitology, and molecular biology.

This important topic was assigned to medical scientist Garang Kuir Ayiik, who has carried out research in the area of health and wellbeing. He started his presentation with a quote in Dinka: 'Ke ye cam, aleu be yin ca pieth guop, kuka leu be yin nok e ya,' loosely translated as 'What you eat can make you look good but can also kill you.' Most diseases that afflict human health are a consequence of the food we eat and the beverages we drink.

Garang explained the importance of community health. When an individual is healthy, the community is healthy as the community is made up of individual members. He defined personal health as being a state of physical, mental, social, and economic wellbeing. Conversely, he defined the absence of health and wellbeing as the presence of diseases, disability, or injury that may lead to death.

On a global scale, the most common diseases are the cardiovascular diseases, followed by infectious diseases and cancers. Garang highlighted common diseases in Africa, many of which are treatable but can still cause death. These include malaria, maternal diseases, and rhoeal diseases. Deaths associated with these illnesses are usually a result of insufficient medication and a low-functioning health system. Garang also highlighted common causes of death in Africa, particularly South Sudan, which included malaria, violence, hunger, maternal and diarrhoeal diseases, and the risk factors for these diseases or conditions. He affirmed that health is a human right and that governments in Africa must spend money to provide universal healthcare to their citizens.

Health and Wellbeing: The Abstract

The health of an individual, community, or nation is defined as a state of complete physical, mental, and social wellbeing. Wellbeing is described as a state of being healthy, happy, and prosperous, having fulfilled or having control over personal, community, or national goals in life; these facets are the integral elements of a thriving community. In practice, pursuits geared towards health and wellbeing focus on an individual member, but access to health services is a shared by all members of a community.

Health and wellbeing are broad topics, but for the purpose of this study, we have explored the global burden of disease to gain an understanding of the nature of diseases and the burdens they pose to populations around the world. Health statistics from the global burden of disease study help us to understand why particular types of diseases are more prevalent in some geographical areas than others— that is, an assessment of their epidemiological distributions on a global scale. Knowledge of prevalence of certain diseases in an area allows stakeholders to plan and streamline delivery of health services.

Moreover, we have also examined healthcare spending. Healthcare expenditure, which varies considerably from country to country and is dependent on the resources of a country or funding agencies, evaluates costs associated with the consumption of healthcare goods and services, including personal healthcare in terms of curative care, rehabilitative care, long-term care, and preventative care, among others.

Furthermore, we have examined the concept of health equity, which informs an important framework in the design and delivery of health systems. Governments, non-governmental organizations, and community- based organizations, such as TECAA, endeavor to provide equal opportunities for all members of a community to access health services whenever and wherever they need them. Health equity is an important concept because health is a fundamental human right.

In conclusion, the members of TECAA should ask this question: How can we make our community a healthy and prosperous community? We shall challenge ourselves to continue to find solutions to pertinent health issues afflicting members of our community, particularly our vulnerable populations in our homeland. This paper provides recommendations, which we hope will lay a foundation for ways to approach and tackle health issues.

Introduction

According to the preamble to the Constitution of the World Health Organization, as adopted by the 1946 International Health Conference, health is defined as 'a state of complete physical, mental, and social wellbeing and not merely the absence of disease or infirmity' (WHO, 1948). In popular discourse, this definition has been criticized as being too idealistic, abstract, and broad, with some experts appealing to include the addition of 'the ability to lead a socially and economically productive life.' However, the definition has remained unchanged since 1948.

While wellbeing is difficult to define because of its inherent multifaceted construct conception, it has been thoroughly described. Wellbeing describes a construct or state of being referring to aspects or states of physical, emotional, psychological, social, or economic being. Attempts to define it have been associated with studies of psychological wellbeing (i.e. happiness) (Dodge, 2012). Several elements that constitute wellbeing have been identified, including autonomy, mastery of one's environment, positive relationships with others, purpose in life, the realization of potential, and self-acceptance (Dodge, 2012). Wellbeing is, therefore, a state of being healthy, happy, and prosperous and having fulfilled or having control over personal [or community or national] goals in life. This description recognizes wellbeing as a state of equilibrium in the continuum of life events. That is, an individual's perception of the balance of positive and negative effects of life events and his or her perceived situational position in this continuum—how well or unwell they feel physically, psychologically, socially, and economically. Wellbeing is, thus, a state of complete meaningful existence. Our perception of our individual health and wellbeing plays an important determining factor in the ways in which we seek healthcare services.

Having explored global burden of diseases and healthcare costs in terms of financial resources needed to fight diseases, the concept of health equity is introduced. Health equity an important framework that informs the design and delivery of health systems. Governments, non-governmental organizations, and community- based organizations, such as TECAA, that are tasked with delivering health services must perform this important function on an equitable basis. All members of a community must be provided with equal opportunities to access healthcare services whenever and wherever they need them. Health equity is an important concept because health is a basic human right of all people.

The Global Burden of Disease
The global burden of disease is a comprehensive epidemiological study that assesses disease mortality, morbidity, and economic burden across diseases, risk factors, and geographical regions. This assessment underscores the impacts of diseases in mortality, disability, economic, and social terms. Economic burdens of disease include loss of productivity time due to infirmity, costs of hospitalization to patients and their families, costs of providing healthcare services in hospitals by governments or non-government organizations, costs of providing care to a sick family member, and loss of social contacts or networks. Burden of disease is an important assessment tool in measuring the impacts of different diseases or disorders and the injuries they cause in a population (AIHW, 2019). Cardiovascular diseases, followed by infectious and parasitic diseases and cancers, are the leading causes of death in the world. Communicable diseases, maternal health complications, and nutritional conditions are the leading causes of death in Africa. These are summarized in a graph in Figure 1 (WHO, 2008).

The first global burden of disease study enumerated the health effects of over one hundred diseases and injuries for eight regions of the world in 1990 (WHO, 2008). The study generated comprehensive and consistent estimates for mortality and morbidity by age, sex, and region. Data generated by such studies provides comprehensive, reliable, and consistent health statistics that are the foundation for evidence-based health policies, strategies, evaluations, and monitoring processes (WHO, 2008).

Figure 1: Distribution of deaths by leading cause groups, males and females in the world (source: WHO, 2004 – updated 2008).

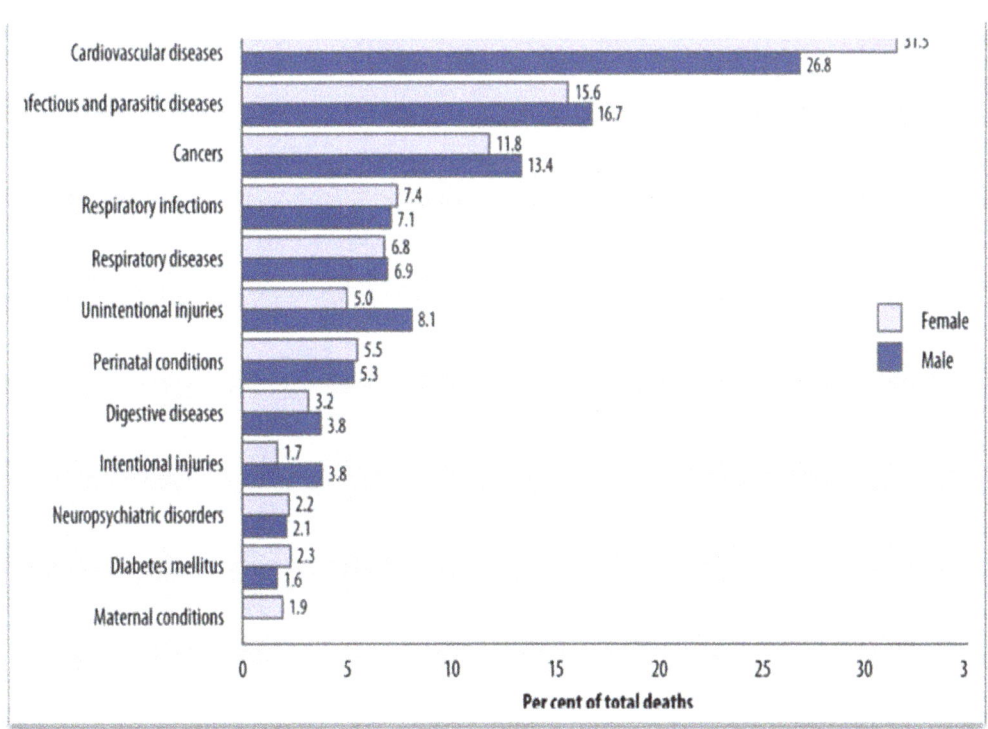

Cause of death statistics as reported by the global burden of disease (GBD) study are sobering. Almost one in five of all deaths in the world occur in children aged under five years. Estimates of annual global deaths in 2004 reported that 58.8 million people died of diseases, conditions, or injuries. Of all the deaths in Africa, 46 percent were children under the age of 15 years. Worldwide, more than half of deaths involved people aged 60 years and over (WHO, 2008). The GBD study categorized diseases and injuries, causes of death, and burdens of diseases into three broad groups. The first group (Group 1) includes communicable, maternal, perinatal, and nutritional diseases. These diseases are generally perceived as poverty diseases. The second group of diseases (Group 2) includes non-communicable diseases, while the third group (Group 3) includes injuries.

Diseases included in group 1, the poverty diseases, are prevalent in developing countries, as illustrated in Table 1.

Table 1. Leading causes of death by income level
(source: WHO, 2008)

	Disease or injury	Deaths (millions)	Per cent of total deaths		Disease or injury	Deaths (millions)	Per cent of total deaths
	World				**Low-income countries[a]**		
1	Ischaemic heart disease	7.2	12.2	1	Lower respiratory infections	2.9	11.2
2	Cerebrovascular disease	5.7	9.7	2	Ischaemic heart disease	2.5	9.4
3	Lower respiratory infections	4.2	7.1	3	Diarrhoeal diseases	1.8	6.9
4	COPD	3.0	5.1	4	HIV/AIDS	1.5	5.7
5	Diarrhoeal diseases	2.2	3.7	5	Cerebrovascular disease	1.5	5.6
6	HIV/AIDS	2.0	3.5	6	COPD	0.9	3.6
7	Tuberculosis	1.5	2.5	7	Tuberculosis	0.9	3.5
8	Trachea, bronchus, lung cancers	1.3	2.3	8	Neonatal infections[b]	0.9	3.4
9	Road traffic accidents	1.3	2.2	9	Malaria	0.9	3.3
10	Prematurity and low birth weight	1.2	2.0	10	Prematurity and low birth weight	0.8	3.2
	Middle-income countries				**High-income countries**		
1	Cerebrovascular disease	3.5	14.2	1	Ischaemic heart disease	1.3	16.3
2	Ischaemic heart disease	3.4	13.9	2	Cerebrovascular disease	0.8	9.3
3	COPD	1.8	7.4	3	Trachea, bronchus, lung cancers	0.5	5.9
4	Lower respiratory infections	0.9	3.8	4	Lower respiratory infections	0.3	3.8
5	Trachea, bronchus, lung cancers	0.7	2.9	5	COPD	0.3	3.5
6	Road traffic accidents	0.7	2.8	6	Alzheimer and other dementias	0.3	3.4
7	Hypertensive heart disease	0.6	2.5	7	Colon and rectum cancers	0.3	3.3
8	Stomach cancer	0.5	2.2	8	Diabetes mellitus	0.2	2.8
9	Tuberculosis	0.5	2.2	9	Breast cancer	0.2	2.0
10	Diabetes mellitus	0.5	2.1	10	Stomach cancer	0.1	1.8

COPD, chronic obstructive pulmonary disease.

Burden of disease is measured in health-adjusted life years (HALYs), an estimate of the combined effects of diseases by measuring their mortality and morbidity in a population, which also allows comparisons across different diseases or disorders or clinical interventions pursued and between populations or sub-populations. Other aspects can also be measured, such as disability-adjusted life years (DALYs), which measure the differences between the current state of health and the ideal life expectancy in a population with 'perfect' health. Time is a critical measure in DALYs; the longer the time of disability, the greater the burden. Quality-adjusted life years (QALYs) measure the quantity and quality of life lived, analyzing the cost effectiveness or efficacy of clinical interventions. Years of life lost (YLL) measure the years of life lost due to premature death—dying before reaching the ideal age of life expectancy. Years lived with disability (YLD) measure years spent living with a disability due to a disease or injury (AIHW, 2019; WHO, 2008).

South Sudan is a country emerging from decades of war and neglect. Health institutions are in their infancy, and consequently, health statistics are imprecise and incomprehensive. No health statistics specific to the Twi East counties were discovered. According to the WHO Sudan's situation report of July 2018, 1.95 million children were vaccinated against measles; 1.78 million people were vaccinated against meningitis; an estimated 261,424 people were reported to be severely malnourished; roughly 0.5 million doses of oral cholera vaccination were deployed; 7 million people, or 47 percent of the pre-2013 war population, were reportedly in dire need of humanitarian assistance; 1.74 million people were internally displaced; and 2.47 million people have sought refuge in neighboring countries (WHO, 2018). Another collaborative report between South Sudan's ministry of health and WHO reported that diarrhoeal diseases, including acute watery diarrhoea and dysentery (bloody diarrhoea), malaria, measles, and parasitic diseases (e.g. visceral leishmaniosis or kala-azar), are the most prevalent diseases in the country (MoH, 2018). Some of these statistics are quite grim. Thus, it's prudent to look at the risk factors for various kind of diseases, not necessarily in the context of South Sudan but as a general overview.

A risk factor is any attribute, characteristic, or exposure that increases an individual's chances of developing a disease or injury (AIHW, 2017). Risk factors for different kinds of diseases exist. Those presented herein are not disease-specific. There are socio-economic factors, such as poverty, poor sanitation, lack of proper housing or overcrowding, human behavior (e.g. alcohol or substance abuse, smoking of tobacco, violence, poor diet, sedentary lifestyle, obesity or weight gain, risky sexual behaviors, and so on), high blood pressure, war, accidental injury, malnutrition, and lack of clean drinking water. There are also environmental or climatic factors, such as poor farming practices, deforestation, industrial waste pollution, air pollution, environmental degradation, floods, unfavorable temperatures, rainfall and humidity, drought, famine, and natural disasters. And there are migration factors, such as international travel and population movements related to displacement during civil unrest or war, epidemics, rural-urban migration, and resettlement.

The Australian burden of disease study (2019) reported percentages of burden of disease attributed to five leading risk factors as shown in Table 2. Behavioral risk factors are those that individuals have control over and could willingly change (AIHW, 2017). From the data presented in Table 2, it is clear that 22.1 percent of cancers and 41 percent of respiratory diseases are caused by tobacco use, while 40.2 percent of cardiovascular diseases and 34.2 percent of endocrine diseases are connected to dietary factors. A staggering 98 percent of endocrine diseases are caused by high plasma glucose. Overweight and obesity are leading risk factors for endocrine, kidney, and urinary diseases and disorders, while high blood pressure is an important risk factor for cardiovascular disease.

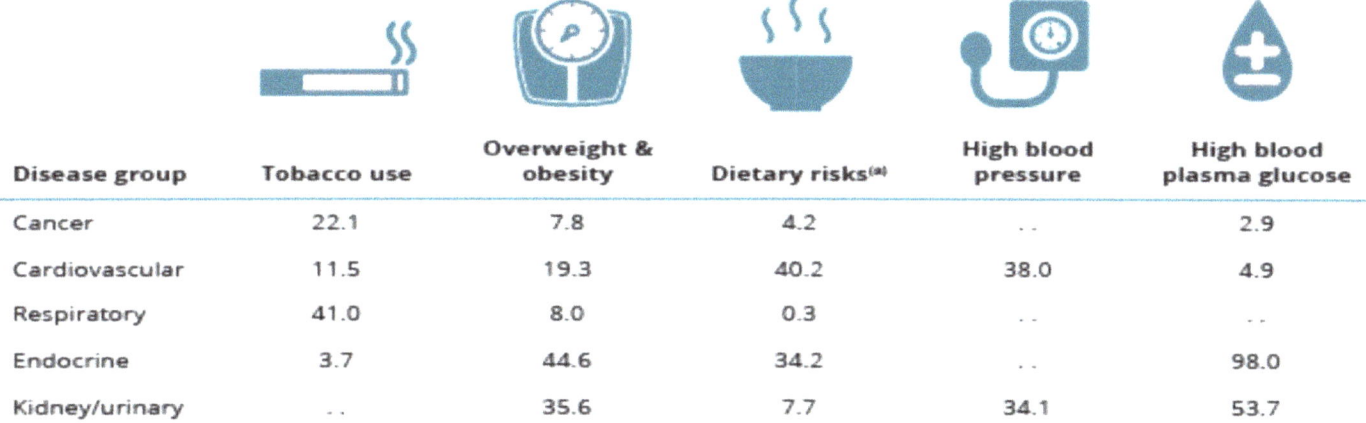

Disease group	Tobacco use	Overweight & obesity	Dietary risks[a]	High blood pressure	High blood plasma glucose
Cancer	22.1	7.8	4.2	. .	2.9
Cardiovascular	11.5	19.3	40.2	38.0	4.9
Respiratory	41.0	8.0	0.3	. .	. .
Endocrine	3.7	44.6	34.2	. .	98.0
Kidney/urinary	. .	35.6	7.7	34.1	53.7

(a) Estimates for diet are based on an analysis of the joint effects of all dietary risk factors included in the study following methods used in recent global burden of disease studies.

Note: Blank cells '. .' indicate that the risk factor has no associated diseases or injuries in the disease group.

Healthcare Spending

Healthcare expenditure varies considerably from country to country and is dependent on the financial resources of a country or funding agencies. Measures of healthcare expenditure evaluate costs associated with the consumption of healthcare goods and services, including personal healthcare in terms of curative care, rehabilitative care, long-term care, preventative care, support services, health administration, and collective services, among others (OECD, 2017; Wieser, 2018). This also includes spending on healthcare goods and services by government (via hospital funding), health insurance, universal medical insurance (e.g. Medicare or Medicaid), capital investment on diagnostic and therapeutic equipment and information and communication systems, and patients' out-of-pocket costs (OECD/WHO, 2018). There is extensive and complex data on healthcare spending, including disease-specific spending. Healthcare spending has been partially or comprehensively categorized by disease for several OECD countries (Wieser, 2018).

Healthcare spending is calculated per capita. The United States is the leading spender per capita of all the OECD countries, in 2016 spending the equivalent of $9,892 USD per person (OECD, 2017). Switzerland ($7,919 USD), Luxembourg ($7,463 USD), Norway ($6,647 USD), and Germany ($5,551 USD) are the next highest spenders. Australia, which ranked at number 13, spent the equivalent of $4,708 USD per capita (OECD, 2017). Health spending is a function of a country's level of wealth, so healthcare spending may be expressed as a percentage of gross domestic product (GDP). Rich or high-income countries spend more on health (OECD/WHO, 2018). Switzerland spends over 80 percent of its healthcare budget on maternal and neonatal services; consequently, it has some of the best outcomes globally for maternal and neonatal health (Wieser, 2018), contributing to Switzerland's high life expectancy. In South Sudan, there is no data on health spending. The bulk of health spending is borne by international NGOs or UN agencies, such as WHO, MSF, LWF, UNICEF, and USAID.

Health Equity and Health Systems

Provision of health services is based on the concept of health equity. Health equity is the provision of equitable opportunities for all people to access health services needed to achieve full health potential. Health equity is defined by the WHO as 'the absence of avoidable, unfair, or remediable differences among groups of people, whether those groups are defined socially, economically, or geographically, or by other means of stratification.' The concept also implies universal health coverage. Universal health coverage is defined as 'all people receiving quality health services that meet their needs without being exposed to financial hardship in paying for the services' (WHO, 2014). The concept of health equity informs modelling of health systems. Health systems, which vary from country to country, should be structured to deliver quality health services to all people whenever and wherever they need them. A robust health system needs:

- Health financing—government, NGOs, social insurance, private fee payment;
- Sufficiently trained and well-paid workforce—doctors, nurses, health support workers, auxiliary staff, laboratory technologists, and so on;
- Well-resourced facilities—hospitals, clinics, super-clinics, and primary health centres; o Medicines;
- Medical equipment and technologies;
- Health policies and therapeutic standards;
- Health information systems (ICT).

Conclusion

In this conference paper, we have examined burdens of diseases to gain an understanding of the nature of diseases that affect human populations around the world. The GBD study offers valuable health statistics, particularly relating to prevalence and incidence of diseases in different geographical regions. These assessment matrices and the epidemiological data gathered on a global scale are invaluable. Knowledge of prevalence of different diseases in an area allows stakeholders to plan relevant health service delivery. This also informs health policy and health decision-making and planning processes.

Having reviewed global burdens of diseases, healthcare spending, and the concepts of health equity and universal health care, it is now appropriate to propose recommendations for the Twi East Communication Association of Australia, an organisation with keen interests in health services-related projects.

Recommendations

- Health project(s) may include provision of equitable, affordable, and accessible healthcare program(s);
- Building of a health facility specialising in certain disease categories;
- A health project that may target specific disease types or a specialty health program (e.g. a mobile eye clinic or a vaccination or immunisation campaign);
- A health program that alleviates socioeconomic health risk factor(s) (e.g. improving sanitation or provision of clean water or providing flood control infrastructure);
- A program that promotes healthy living (e.g. a nutritional program or child feeding centre);
- A program that creates awareness (e.g. an antimicrobial stewardship program or zoonotic control program);

- Partnership with other NGOs or government departments in support of specific health programs;
- Creation of sustainable healthy communities;
- Response to a legal loophole by establishing a body to oversee the executive's activities. This will ensure amicable resolution of any potential conflict if the Executive Committee fails to comply with specific stipulations of the constitution. The body will be appointed by the General Assembly with the help of either state or county leaders.

These are a few potential functions:
- Liaise with the Executive Committee to shape the operational framework of the association.
- Work together with the Executive Committee to gauge achievements, opportunities, and challenges and devise a mechanism to strategically resolve challenges;
- Ensure that the Executive Committee operates within the policies and constitution of the association and Australian laws;
- Assist the Executive Committee in conducting internal audits and ensure that approved budgets are accurately executed/implemented;
- Together with the Executive Committee, ensure that all members respect the values and direction of the association;
- When needed, monitor the performance of the Executive Committee and gauge its success against the strategic direction set for the association;
- Provide advice and, when needed, guidance to the Executive Committee and assist in facilitating electoral processes;
- Call for a meeting of the General Assembly when the Executive Committee's term of office expires and appoint an electoral committee to organise elections.

Organizational Successes and Challenges

By Joseph Garang Deng and David Deng Amol

The two gentlemen tasked with this research are Joseph Garang Deng and David Deng Amol. The team expressed their appreciation for the opportunity to contribute towards charting the path of the great community of Twi East. They briefly outlined the definition of an association, explaining how an association can be formed by five or more members based on the needs identified by the group.

They listed the Australian states and territories in which members of the Twi East community reside. Twi East members have organised themselves into state/territory based organisations.

The team articulated that TECAA has important benefits for members of the Twi East community in Australia. Some of the benefits listed were:

- The association helps in mobilizing ideas and resources for the betterment of the community.
- The association enables members to interact with other members in different parts of the world.
- The association allows Western values and democracy (secret ballots), linking Twi East people to Western ways life.
- The association preserves the cultures of Twi East people in Australia through cultural programs.

The team also informed the conference about some challenges that the association is facing. The following challenges were listed:

- Difficulties in bringing young people up in a culturally appropriate manner due to negative environmental factors in Australia.
- Insults directed at leaders who voluntarily contribute their time, causing a lack of respect for our leaders. Institutions that are built with a culture of individual and institutional respect prosper and stand the test of time. As leaders are volunteers, all we can pay them is our respect for their time and values.
- Difficulties in organizing regular meetings and cultural events due to geographical distribution of community members in Australia.
- New Western values—for instance, election processes. Elections sometimes present challenges to our members as they are conducted through secret ballots, causing suspicion after results are announced.
- Different laws and regulations in different states and territories, discrepancies posing a threat to the association. The team recommended that the association be registered with ASIC;
- Insufficient ties between TECAA and county associations. The team also identified some threats facing the association:
- Lack of commitment from members due to their commitments to their county associations.

- Social media trolling, lowering moral and discouraging members from volunteering their time and expertise.

Furthermore, the team identified and recommended some steps to address some of the challenges and threats identified above:
- Leadership should establish good relationships with local organizations and authorities so that TECAA can attract more assistance from experts and funding bodies.
- The association should work hard and encourage young people to learn about the values and ways of life of Twi East people. This should be done via the Twi East community state-based associations.
- The term of the office should be increased from two years to three years, allowing the executive office to plan, consult, and implement programs with greater ease.
- Future elections should be conducted differently. Members should only elect the president of the association, then authorize the president to form his/her executive body. This will allow the president to determine the office bearers based on their capabilities and expertise, and it will also prevent power wrangling in the office.

TECAA was formed in 2009 in New South Wales. Twi East associations operate where Twi East people live in large numbers and where such associations are legally incorporated. TECAA is now registered and incorporated in most major Australian cities. The states and territories are represented in Twi federal leadership. The payam associations and TECAA coordinate security issues jointly. They also coordinate matters relating to natural disasters and humanitarian needs that affect our people in Twi land. TECAA responds to road projects, dams, floods, and other Twi community issues, while payam associations focus on building schools and health centres in their counties, payams, and Boma.

TECAA brings Twi East people together from around the globe through conferences and meetings. The association mobilises diverse ideas in a pool for the common vision of the association. It helps to address humanitarian issues faced by Twi East people in Australia and at home, generating funds through donations and fundraisers. TECAA helps with the development of Twi land by raising funds for infrastructure, such as roads and dams. It liaises with other Twi subsidiaries/branches in the US, Canada, and East Africa to communicate matters of insecurity caused by external attacks on our people in Twi land. The association promotes values of Western democracy and human rights among our people in Australia and works to preserve our cultures and values by performing cultures during gatherings.

The geographical distribution of our people throughout Australia affects service delivery and message coordination. The adoption of processes and values of Western democracy as a way of managing our association can cause difficulties in understanding of the rights and obligations of and to the incorporated association. Different interpretations and applications of state and territory acts affect members' comprehension of the operation of the association within the law. Questions of accountability and transparency by TECAA leadership in managing the funds of the association may incite doubts among financial members.
- Lack of willing members who can serve the association on a voluntary basis
- Lack of community attachment and relationships with the wider Australian society

Crises in *Payams* and state and territory associations affect communication between TECAA leadership and the people in those jurisdictions. Threats to Payam associations sometimes translate into lack of commitment by the same members to serve Twi associations at federal level.
- Ideological attachment under different names by our people and community threaten the existence of Twi East as an entity.
- Economic fluctuations affect financial capability of members to fund the association.
- Improper use of social media affects the association.
- Failure to follow the requirements of the acts of fair-trade affects legality.
- Some Western cultures undermine the values and cultures of Twi East.

There is a need for TECAA to conform to the Fair Work Agreement and the rules of incorporated associations, particularly when it comes to financial reporting and management of the association.

Recommendations
- Link: There is a great need for TECAA's leaders to double their efforts in establishing good working relationships with governments, government agencies, and non-governmental organisations in Australia to improve service delivery to members across the country.
- Purpose: TECAA should devote time and energy to devising an effective way to explain to its members, especially young members, the core reasons for the association's existence and the things that must be done to ensure that it achieves its objectives. This can be done at a grass root level in states and territories, where gatherings are organised mainly to discuss these issues with regard to the achievements and future of TECAA.
- Mechanism: TECAA would be better managed if the chairman was given the power to allocate portfolios, such as treasury, to members nominated by the states and territories. This would promote control and discipline in leadership.
- Reward: Reward can be seen in two different ways. First, once the association has achieved its objectives, TECAA will become a prosperous, united association that will co-exist peacefully with its neighbours in the diaspora and in Jonglei State in South Sudan. Second, rewards for TECAA members in Australia will include advocacy roles for TECAA on behalf of its members in areas such as social security, employment, education, and sporting issues, as well as wellbeing of Australia members.
- Legal loopholes must be addressed by establishing a body to oversee the executive's activities. This will ensure amicable resolution of any potential conflicts if the Executive Committee fails to comply with specific stipulations of the constitution. The body will be appointed by the General Assembly with the help of state or county leaders.

Potential functions of the proposal committee:
- Liaise with the Executive Committee to shape the operational framework of the association;
- Work with the Executive Committee to gauge achievements, opportunities, and challenges and devise a mechanism to strategically resolve those challenges;
- Ensure that the Executive Committee operates within the policies and constitution of the association and Australian laws;
- Assist the Executive Committee in conducting internal audits and ensure that approved budgets are accurately executed/implemented;
- Work with the Executive Committee to ensure that all members respect the values and direction of the association;
- Monitor the performance of the Executive Committee, gauging its success against the strategic direction set for the association;
- Provide advice and guidance to the Executive Committee and assist in facilitating electoral processes;
- Call for a General Assembly meeting when the Executive Committee's term of office expires to appoint an electoral committee to organise elections.

Questions
'As a member of Twi East Community Association in Australia, what kind of relationship would you like to see between TECAA and Twi East Payam associations in Australia?'

'If TECAA becomes a tax-deductible gift/donation recipient organization in Australia, will such an arrangement encourage you, as a member, to make more gifts/donations to TECAA, knowing that you will get the money back when you do your tax return at the end of the financial year?'

'As a member of TECAA, can you share with us the real and perceived challenges faced by the Twi community in the diaspora and at home?'

Akoi Bol led discussion of Part E

PART E: Speeches and Discussions

The conference was well organised, and the program was well balanced. Presentations from Twi experts provided a good background about the needed elements for TECAA, and speakers delivered good overviews of potential solutions to barriers faced by the association.

Experienced speakers delivered outstanding messages, summarizing the core objectives of the conference. Below are a few key takeaways recorded during the two-day conference. The people who delivered these messages are experts who were invited to speak.

Keynote Address 1

By Philip Aguer Panyang (Former Governor of Jonglei State)

As the head of the delegation from Africa, Hon Philip Aguer was welcomed to the stage by the president of the association and met with a standing ovation and some historic revolutionary songs of the mighty SPLA by TECAA members. Aguer started his speech by greeting and thanking the community for the warm welcome. He noted that the invitation to attend the reunion meant a great deal to him, even more than his appointment as the governor of Jonglei State.

'My warm greetings to all of you. Also, my congratulations to you for being able to mobilise and organise such a great and very important forum. I must thank you for inviting me to attend as one of you, who think constantly about our country, our people, our state, our counties, and our payams and Boma as the most backward places of the world. I appreciate you for inviting me to contribute ideas and suggestions on how best we can collectively contribute to supporting development of our home.

'Exactly one year ago, I was sent to the US by the Greater Bor leadership as a governor of Jonglei State to brief them about many issues at home, and some of you heard my speeches online. I am more than happy to open my speech to this important gathering of Twi East people with a few statements about the entire country, as you are from the inner set of the subset of South Sudan, before I concentrate on Twi land, which is the focus of the conference.

'Today, I address some of the issues from one year ago. Socio-economic dynamism might have brought its own differences in form and content, and to me, it is on the positive side for Twi and for South Sudan. Some things are blessings in disguise, and some things are direct blessing.

'First, from the perspective of peace for South Sudan, my expectations for peace are much higher this time than a year ago. The factors for these hopes are the visit of the key actors after signing the revitalized peace agreement to Rome and the washing and kissing of the feet of President Kiir Mayardit, Dr Riek Machar, and Rebecca Nyandeng by the Pope. This drew attention of the international community, showing that the people of South Sudan deserved peace, as expressed by the Pope, who represents God on Earth.

'Secondly, the fall of Beshier and the change of guards in Khartoum might lead to a change of ideology and approach to relations with the South in Khartoum.

'Thirdly, the regional actors, especially Ethiopia and Uganda, will be more engaged in their internal affairs in the coming period.

'Fourthly, the people of South Sudan are tired of wars and may be reluctant to support another bloody war. Even if some selfish politicians want to use war for personal gain, it will be like the end of a rainy season, when you will hear some sporadic thunder but no actual rain. Many people in South Sudan are praying to God to listen to the majority and not to a small group for the sake of peace.

'These are the basis of my hope that this time we have more hopes for peace in South Sudan. Though predictions are more accurate in natural sciences than in social sciences, we must plan from a high moral ground that if all actors, local, national, regional, and international, do the right things, we can secure lasting peace in South Sudan.

'Again, peace requires sacrifice, forgiveness, and reconciliation. Brothers and sisters, today as I address Twi community, my belief in peace and unity of the people of South Sudan is the basis for my commitment to the unity of our people in Twi East and in Jonglei State.

'Dear brothers and sisters, before I go into the topics and answer the questions framed by the organising committee, let me first state the main challenges facing our people at home. These challenges can be divided into chronic challenges and transient or emerging challenges.

Chronic challenges:
- Lack of roads and the consequences of this
- Lack of equipment in hospitals/clinics and the consequences of this
- Shortage of medical doctors/nurses and the consequences of this
- Seasonal floods and the consequences of these

How do we mitigate and reduce the impact of the above challenges on the lives of our people?
These challenges require:
- Sizable budget
- Long-term solutions
- Both private and public sector involvement
- Strong will and commitment

Transient or emerging challenges:
- Insecurity both politically motivated and locally generated, like cattle raiding and child abduction;
- Shortage of clean drinking water affecting health;
- Lack of surveys in boma, payams, and county settlements;
- Lack of markets to encourage movement of people for sale and purchase of goods;
- River blockages affecting fishing and river transport;
- Lack of an accessible river port;
- Lack of sustainable communication systems connecting all the boma and payams of Twi; East counties;
- Erosion or loss of traditional cultures.

Most of these challenges require:
- Less budget
- Short-term solutions
- Public consensus to find solutions and prepare interventions

All of these challenges are intended to generate discussion by the participants of the conference. Those who have lived them may suggest ideas for moving forward. Our approach here should be people-to-people development.

'I am honoured and delighted by this invitation to visit you in Australia and share news, challenges, and expectations in our country, the place of your birth. I am also aware that those who were born in the diaspora are forming the second generation of diaspora citizens and deserve correct information so that they can realistically participate in shaping the future South Sudan.'

Aguer thanked the Twi East community for its support when he became governor, and he acknowledged Twi East people in Bor-town, Juba, and Australia. He reiterated what Canon Mark Atem said earlier about the people of Jonglei State who are scattered around the globe acting as a sign of love from God. This is also what Bishop Nathaniel Garang Anyieth said: God has a purpose for His people.

Aguer referenced what Rev Ateny said in one of the funeral prayers in Juba. He declared that people who have spoken directly to God are four: Moses, Elijah, Elisha, and Dr John Garang. He continued that in 1985, when the Koryom battalion was graduated, a dream came to a man called Pach from Bioong in Bonga, Ethiopia. In the dream, Pach saw an airplane that was carrying Dr John Garang crash into a mountain. He was later taken to the headquarters to narrate the dream to Garang. Garang responded with a big smile and told Pach not to worry, saying that the dream was true but would be far off, the crash not to happen until after the southerners had achieved their objective. The event occurred exactly as it had in the dream 20 years later.

Aguer acknowledged the leaders, elders, and community members for coming together to create practical programs for the community. He stated that all the liberators in African history were once in the diaspora. Since the country has already been liberated, the primary task of South Sudanese people in the diaspora now is to contribute to nation building.

He emphasized the importance of education, particularly the value of vocational education. He drove home the point by telling the story of a friend who dropped out of high school but went to Saudi Arabia, where he gained more resources and knowledge than those who were still pursuing their dreams through formal education.

Keynote Address 2 – Community Structures

By Hon Isaiah Chol Aruai

Isaiah Chol Aruai advised the Twi East community to first focus on organising the community in Australia before all focusing their attention on the community back at home, saying that the community will only be effective in helping Twi East people in South Sudan once they have streamlined their efforts and adopted proper community structures. For instance, there is no South Sudan embassy in Australia, something the community must work hard to remedy. When Australia and South Sudan have a good working relationship, it will be much easier to live as citizens of the two countries.
Women's Empowerment
Aruai also told the community that women will need to be included in committees to ensure that they are empowered.

Helping people back home: Hon. Chol appreciated the effort of the Diaspora community in pulling resources together to help the people of Twi East community in Twi land and South Sudan in general during these difficult times. He encouraged the community to continue with this spirit of being the source of life for their relatives and friends in Africa during search difficult time. He stated that once peace comes to South Sudan then the load being shouldered by the diaspora community will reduce significantly as relatives and friends who work in South Sudan will be able to contribute towards the cost of living for your relatives and friends.

Helping People Back Home
Aruai acknowledged the efforts of the diaspora community in pulling resources together to help the people of the Twi East community in Twi land, and South Sudan in general, during these difficult times. He encouraged the community to continue with this spirit of being a source of life for relatives and friends in Africa. He stated that once peace comes to South Sudan, the load being shouldered by the diaspora community will reduce significantly as relatives and friends who work in South Sudan will be able to contribute towards their own cost of living.

Road Project
Aruai appreciated the courage of Twi East people in the diaspora who plan and consult about important projects to better the lives of people back home. He argued that leaders should be clear about which projects are meant to be done by the government of South Sudan and which can be carried out by local communities. No matter how weak the government is, there are projects that the community cannot do without federal assistance.
An example is the road, which is a public good that the government should be responsible for. Aruai respectfully disagreed with the road project, stating that 1 km of paved road will cost around 1 million US dollars. He jokingly asked the audience, 'How many km of road do you want to construct in the Twi East area?' He warned the community not to work on public goods like roads that should be the responsibility of the government.

Divorce
Aruai talked about how difficult divorce is in Dinka culture. He told the community that men pay high dowry prices to marry their wives and spend more to bring them to Australia. This is a lifetime investment for men, so women should not just kick their husbands out of their houses for the sake of it. He told women that elders organise marriages in South Sudan, and despite Australian practices, to elders in Africa, those married in South Sudan will remain so, at least culturally. He spoke about high bride prices, saying that they are the making of the diaspora community and encouraging marriage of girls in the diaspora. He asked the community why many people go to Africa to find brides when there are many beautiful girls here in Australia.

Youth Issues
Aruai spoke about the situation of young people in Australia. Sometimes, parents make a desperate move, taking their children back to Africa if they have started to misbehave and break the law in Australia. When children are taken back to South Sudan, there is nothing that the South Sudanese community can do for them. Aruai encouraged parents to take their children back to Africa while they can still be rehabilitated, not later when nothing can be done for them.

Aruai told the conference that how children grow largely depends on their parents' level of investment in them. He asked parents to spend more time with their children, building strong relationships to encourage their children to confide in them. Youth issues of our community can be mitigated by what parents and community groups do to help young people.

Unity
Aruai also talked about the importance of unity in the community. He encouraged the Twi East community to ensure that all members act part of a big picture in the community, remaining united regardless of differing opinions on community progress. He acknowledged the importance of the Twi East community Council of Elders and jokingly said that he hoped it wouldn't become like the Jieng Council of Elders in Juba. The Council of Elders will help leadership steer the community in the right direction.

Census

Aruai commended the leaders of the Twi East community in Australia for having conducted a census to identify the number of members in Australia. He stated that planning and implementation of programs is only possible when the exact number of members being serviced is known. He informed the conference that the population of the Twi East community globally is nearly 130,000. But these people are scattered widely, the majority of them living in refugee camps and in the diaspora, leaving a very small number of people in the Twi East area back home. Our people must be encouraged to return home by incentives like food security, education, and health facilities.

Term of Office

Aruai advised Australia's Twi East community to amend the constitution and extend the term of the office to four years instead of two, agreeing with the recommendation made by Garang Deng and Deng Amol to increase the term of office. He explained that two years is too short to give the Executive Committee time to implement programs. He left his recommendation on the matter in the constitutional review process. He then acknowledged those who have conducted research on selected topics.

Keynote Address 3

By Hon Ayiei Manyok Ajak

My dear brothers and sisters in Australia and all over the globe, it is my pleasure to have this golden chance to meet with you here today in the very historical town of Melbourne, Australia.

'In Twi East, currently, we have schools, health centres, humanitarian organisations, churches, and businesses that are operational. The population in every Payam is living in his/her ancestral land, and that is from Mar to Wernyol.

The major challenges we are facing are as follows:
- Insecurity is rampant, mainly from neighbouring states of Boma, Biech, Fangak, and Eastern Lakes. This rampant insecurity has led to high rates of poverty in the area, whereby people have no accessibility to farming and cattle rearing within the territory of Twi East.
- Educational centres are not in a standard form due to the current economic crisis in South Sudan, and that has led to poor quality education in the area.
- Health centres are lacking facilities due to poor road networks in the country and inactive support from health partners, so death rates are increasing.
- Humanitarian organisations are not doing their activities very well. They are needed by dense populations in areas of Twi East, but poor roads lead to inaccessibility.
- Land disputes have become a major challenge in the area, and they have led to loss of trust among the communities.
- Flooding has become a major challenge. As you know, Twi East is a lowland area. This leads to the overflow of water from the River Nile to inhabited land, affecting crops and livestock.
- Another challenge is child abductions, which have become a major problem in Twi East and in other areas of Jonglei State. I hope that all of you are aware of the scenarios, since you have been there. But the problem has still not been addressed by our current government, and it has become a serious matter.
- Communication networks are too poor, causing communication gaps between ourselves and those who are in the diaspora.

Recommendations

'I am very much interested in sharing with you my recommendations. My recommendations are as follows:

- We, the sons and daughters of Twi East, need to put our hands together to solve the issue of insecurity. This needs human capital and financial resources to motivate the youth currently guarding the community.
- We must put peace first. We are from one family, one geographical area with common characteristics. This will bring our community to live in harmony.
- We need to work together to improve the health situation for our sisters and brothers who are living in poor health conditions back home.
- We should encourage our families to return home for better development. There is no development without population.
- I encourage knowledgeable people and well-wishers to come up with NGOs and take them to Twi East for operation. This will promote education for our children and other development programs.
- We must reclaim lands that have been covered by water since 1988, pushing the dyke to the west, as indicated in the map.

To conclude, I am very happy to attend this reunion conference. I encourage you to remember your homeland first in any activity you plan. I advise you not to think of the past but of how far you have come. I encourage you to visit your home at any time you wish. I believe we will achieve what we need if we work together.

In case of any questions or queries concerning Twi East affairs, do not hesitate to ask me. I wish you good luck for our bright future.

Keynote Address 4

By Benjamin Bul Duom (Member of Council of Elders) and Ador Akechnhial

The member of the Council of Elders Benhamin Bul Duom began by asking all members to participate in the name of our Lord Jesus Christ, who is the same yesterday, today, and tomorrow.

He acknowledged that there are major problems that have been faced by the entire Twi area, as well as other areas, for the last 60 years and continue to be faced today. In order to solve insecurity in the Twi area, he suggested unity among Twi area occupants: Lith, Kongor, Nyuak, Ajuong, and Pakeer.

How to achieve unity:
- Five-person conflict management committee (one representative from each Payam)
- Five political monitors (one representative from each Payam)

Their duties should be to investigate current and future needs of the Twi area, to identify common good, and to achieve demands such as:
- Community engagement methods to support proposed plans. If the above objectives are fulfilled, the whole Twi area will easily achieve unity based on the needs of the community. Twi must also establish good relations with other communities and neighbours;
- To also work with the aim of achieving political and economic progress;
- Combat fear and insecurity by establishing a joint campaign with both Duken (Hold and Nyarweng) to make settlements in the Gadiang area, working to combat other problems faced by the Twi area, including hunger, insecurity, lack of paved roads, and insufficient schools and health centres.

Also, he stated that all roads ought to lead to Gadiang. How can this be achieved? All costs and problems should be shouldered by each area.
- For Duken, from Patal to Gadiang
- Payoom to Gadiang (fuel payable by Lith)
- Piol to Gadiang (fuel payable by Ajuong and Pakeer)

By working to achieve the above, he stated that there will be no hunger or insecurity, that schools will be built and health centres will be established, and that the whole area will live in peace, dancing together, eating together, and engaging in inter-marriage at low costs. At the end of his speech, he said, 'I would like to give my great thanks to all of you for coming today and giving me the opportunity to speak.'

Keynote Address 5

By Ajang Diing Awuol (Twi East Youth Leader, Juba)

Twi East Youth President in Australia Chol Akech introduced his counterpart from Juba, welcoming him to the stage to address the conference. Ajang Diing Awuol was welcomed to the stage with a song. He has been praised for his good deeds as a Twi East youth leader in Juba. He started his speech by thanking the current Executive Committee and the president for the invitation to attend the conference and for the good work they do to improve the lives of Twi East people.

Awuol emphasized the need for the Twi East community to remain united and to cooperate at all levels. He spoke about how the Twi East symbol was chosen and the significance it carries for the people of Twi East. He suggested that the Twi East community will need to properly coordinate projects so that one project is active at a time and our efforts can be concentrated, enabling us to see projects through to completion.

As part of his campaign promises, Awuol has found land to build a Twi East youth compound in Shirkat, Juba. The youth association in South Sudan contributed towards this project, but the project cannot proceed at this stage. Awuol asked the Twi East community in Australia to contribute towards establishing a fence around the land.

Awuol thanked the community members for contributing immensely towards maintaining the lives of relatives and friends in East Africa, and he asked the diaspora community to support peace in South Sudan through their social media interactions, helping all parties involved in the revitalized peace agreement to remain committed to peace implementation in South Sudan.

Awuol offered to talk to members of the Twi East community in Australia if there are people experiencing conflict. He expressed his profound gratitude for the contributions of the late Abiol Atem, who tirelessly trained young people in Melbourne in traditional dance. He also asked that women begin to play a greater role in reshaping the direction of our community.

TEYAA President Chol Akech

Keynote Address 6

by State/Territory Leaders Representative

State and territory leaders were represented by the chairperson of Twi East community in Western Australia, Majok Jawat, who introduced his colleagues from the other states. He emphasised the need to retain Twi East's rural population by establishing conducive work environments and taking towns to the Twi East area to prevent our people from migrating to capital cities.

Keynote Address 7

By County Representatives

County representatives were represented by Thuch Atem, deputy president of the Ajuong community. He thanked the organisers for putting a remarkable event together. He encouraged the Twi East community to remain united and to cooperate on issues of development to take our community to the next level.

Keynote Address 8

By Akech Dau Angok on Behalf of the New State Proposal Committee

Akech Dau Angok spoke briefly about the importance of the Twi East area having its own state. He highlighted the importance of having a new state, linking the idea to historical armed struggles in South Sudan, community interest, unfair distribution of resources in the current state, insecurity, and support of SPLM's vision.

Benefits of State Security

Akech believes that a new state will create more public jobs—2 parliaments with 42 MPs in Jonglei and Bor will be needed, along with 2 governors and 14 cabinet members, each with several staff. It will also provide equitable and viable county allocation, contribute to advances in national government seats, address census imbalances in the current state, lessen unhealthy rivalries in current Jonglei, support businesses and NGOs, and reduce migration. Akech said that these factors would also relate to other important sectors, including development, economy, and moral and social aspiration.

Keynote Address 9

Speakers spoke passionately about development and unity among the people of Twi East, helping to achieve their potential, and thanked the leaders of the Twi East community who invited them to Melbourne.

Part F: Viewpoints

A) Agriculture Food Uncertainty

By Elijah Dau Wer, Jonglei Food Security CEO

Today, Twi East people are faced by high rates of insecurity and food shortages. In terms of food security, Twi East ranks as one of the hungriest countries in the Jonglei State, with an estimated half of the population needing food assistance. According to Jonglei Food Security's (JFS) latest update on food insecurity in Twi East areas, a quarter or more of the population is facing crisis or emergency levels of hunger, and these are far from being the only areas flagged as cause for concern. The largest population is now in IDP crisis, including people coping with acute hunger in refugee camps in neighbouring countries.

Serious food security concerns have been overshadowed by crises in other parts of Twi East, and the situation is rapidly deteriorating. Indeed, the intensification of insecurity is a key reason behind the recent resurgence of Twi East hunger levels following decades of steady declines. The war of 2013 caused food insecurity, starvation, and malnutrition. An examination of the three counties JFS operates in—Bor South, Twi East, and Duk—indicated that 137,000 people in Bor South, 93,000 people in Twi East, and 90,000 people in Duk are food insecure.

Dau Wer acknowledged that there are many risks at any time in the area. For instance:
- Protecting crops from animals, thieves, and fires is difficult. The likelihood of poverty is medium, and the impact is high, but there may be some solutions that could encourage people to return to their ancestral homes.
- In Twi East, there is rivalry of leadership, and this causes political conflict, leading to war. The government in Jonglei should ensure that law and order are applied to all violent groups, and crop fences should be deployed to protect crops from damage.
- Seasonal floods, drought, and heat are of medium likelihood in the Twi area. The solution is to build a dyke to prevent flooding from entering farms and to build a sewage linking system to Jonglei Canal.
- Insects in the area have a medium likelihood of affecting crops. Farmers should ensure that herbicides are applied to prevent diseases.

The solution to the above-mentioned causes is to restore hope through agriculture and food production.

Dau Wer suggested alternative solutions to cattle rustling and child abduction issues in former Jonglei State, proposing peace through financial punishment or collective punishments, as opposed to individual punishment. It is not the first time such a tough law has been used. This was the strategy used Anglo-Egyptian Chief C. A. Wills, who later became the first Upper Nile Province governor under British rule. The strategy eradicated sectional war in many parts of South Sudan. If mediators between Buma State and neighbouring states need an easy solution, we have to consider these strategies, which are as follows:

- Compensation for helicopters, monitoring, and verification must be taken from the invader's state's budget in cases of murder, stolen or killed cows, or damaged property. It is the responsibility of the home state of law-breakers to punish its own criminals by tracing them and demanding reimbursement for the amount taken from the state budget.
- A Joined Forces for Verification and Monitoring (JFVM) team must be formed to gather reports of attacks.
- 10 members from each state should be witnesses of incident reviews and should report back to the Joined Compensation Financial Team (JCFT) to arrange compensation for the affected state.
- All governors must sign this agreement.
- 75 percent of JFVM must identify and agree on the origin state of attackers, acquiring this information by monitoring them on helicopter and on foot and recording how many people have been killed and how many cows have been stolen or killed in crossfire and assessing the costs of damaged properties.

JCFT will be responsible for payments of compensation to the invaded state(s) from the budget of invaders' state. Only letting each state carry its own cross or applying strategies to attempt to stop raiders can put an end to cattle rustling and child abduction.

To achieve sustainable development and food security and nutrition goals, steps to support resilient livelihoods must be combined with peacebuilding and conflict resolution efforts. Investing in food security can strengthen efforts to prevent hunger and poverty and achieve sustained peace.

B) Improving Security in Jonglei:
Local Community Response to Insecurities in the Region

By Deng from Nairobi

Dear communities of Jonglei and specially Jieng communities of Duk, Twic East, Athooc and Gok. We dream everyday of living in a safe and secure areas in Jonglei state with no threats of your cattle being raided and no child being abducted by unknown criminals however, we are more exposed to our long standing problems in our area like never before. The safety and mobility of our people and goods are greatly in danger. Our life expectancy in the region is getting lower and lower at 30s, chronic hunger is at everyone doorstep bringing about extreme malnutrition to both adults and children at alarming rates with local population depending donor's aid every year. Fear is constant while news of people getting killed in the villages by raiding criminals is an order of the day. With national government unresponsive to its citizens' problems and the state government with limited capacity to tackle our challenges, it is time for us to put our brain and resources together for our own safety and welfare.

Rifle conflicts and attacks in Jonglei
Over many decades we have faced together the worst threats in Jonglei hence scattering many and leading to loss of many lives as well. These threats remain alive and increased today and include but are not limited or exclusive to:
1. Attacks on villages from neighbouring communities coupled with cattle rustling/raiding, killing and abduction of children e.g. from Murle
2. Seasonal floods every year (I will tackle this topic in another article)
3. Highway attacks
4. Chronic hunger brought about by insecurity as farmers cannot safely engage in farming in their communities.
5. Poor infrastructure such as muddy feeder roads within Jonglei areas.
6. Lack of social amenities e.g. lack of electricity
7. Lack of children access to quality education
8. Environmental problems such as degradation of environments due to lack of protective environmental policies. Deforestation, bushfires that emits too much carbon into air hence leading to health problems.

Due to the stated problems above, it is sad to say that the life expectancy is so low at 35 years in Jonglei. Deadly and bloodiest cattle rustlings are endemic, presence of small arms and weaponized communities have put the lives of their residents at risks as small arguments may lead to gunfights any time. Non- enforcement of strict rule of law as well as use of traditional court system are also endangering lives of many people in the areas of Jonglei state.

Community based surveillance strategy
With our government unable to give protection to the citizen who are at risks, it is high time we shift in to defend lives which are at stake in our vulnerable communities.

To tackle the above interlinked problems, I prefer to address the clause of insecurity because once there is no insecurity, all others can be solved with ease.

Principally, there are two layers of security to address:
- Security at national government level and
- Security at the state government level

In this article, I want to focus on how to tackle insecurity at the state level which is what will address insecurities at the Buma and Counties levels by proposing the following aggressive modern security strategies:
1. The state government should mark red spots (danger zones), these are places that continually receive multiple attacks every year and are highly vulnerable. These places initially had dense population

and little security presence though their population dwindled due to constant attacks they received. Preferably, these red spots could be identified behind the following communities: Duk, Twic East, Athooc, and Gok. After marking those red spots, security presence in terms of police or army outposts need to be put in those places to protect the communities and their properties.
2. Community authorities need to establish Community Rapid response team stationed at strategic locations within the community which would quickly respond to eminent attack on their community in time.
3. State government (or communities) need to employ use of drones and CCTV in the forests to help in identifying moving criminals and to alert communities for possible attacks on them. To do this, state government (or communities) need to mobilize resources from its residents, citizens in diaspora and cooperate with donors abroad in getting the needed equipment, trainings and maintenance. Centers at strategic locations must be identified to function as security control points in surveillance, coordinating and alerting the authorities and community residents of a possible danger cited. If those in diaspora can be contributing let's say a $100 per month per person and there are 200,000 able people contributing monthly, then it would amount to $ 240,000,000 annually apart from local government funds, hence can adequately finance the security operational programs of the project.

This article is exhaustive; therefore, further opinions are welcome to improve it.

Part G: Appendix

Appendix A) Conference Evaluation Form

We would like to hear from conference participants about what you liked and what you didn't like at this conference. Please take a minute to answer the evaluation from of this event.

Circle one. Poor 1,2, 3. Good 4, 5. Very Good 6, 7, 8. Excellent 9,10.

1. Conference site arrangement 1 2 3 4 5 6 7 8 9 10
Comments _____

2. Opening program 1 2 3 4 5 6 7 8 9 10
Comments _____

3. Special AGM Proceeding 1 2 3 4 5 6 7 8 9 10
Comments _____

4. Topic: General discussion 1 2 3 4 5 6 7 8 9 10
Comments _____

5. Speaker: General Keynote Speakers 1 2 3 4 5 6 7 8 9 10
Comments _____

6. Overall Quality of Presentation 1 2 3 4 5 6 7 8 9 10
Comments _____

7. Conference Papers designed 1 2 3 4 5 6 7 8 9 10
Comments _____

8. Was the purpose of the conference clear to you when you attended? Yes / No / Somewhat
Comments _____

9. What were you looking for from the conference? New Ideas / Networking / New Approach / Other
If "other," please describe _____

10. Did you find what you were expecting for? Yes / No / Somewhat
Comments _____

11. What did you enjoy most about the conference? _____

12. What did you enjoy least? _____

13. Is there anything else you would like us to know about the conference?

_____

Appendix A) Conference Evaluation Form

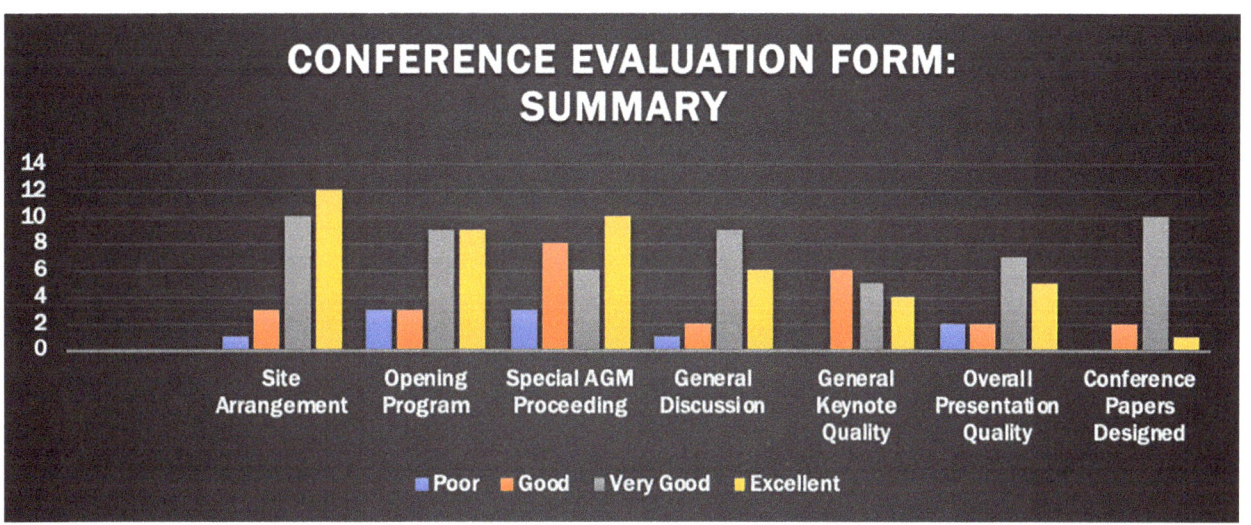

Evaluation Summary

General Comments
- Overall, the area with the highest satisfaction rate was site arrangement.
- The area with the lowest satisfaction rate was the overall quality of the presentation.

This summary of the conference evaluation form suggests that results were largely mixed, some attendees rating satisfaction extremely high, others extremely lowly. The category with the most consistent results was the special AGM proceeding; satisfaction mostly ranged from good to excellent.

Notable comments from open questions in the survey:
- 'Conference agendas should be distributed to Twi East members through their state branches before any conference.'
- 'Speeches were too long.'
- 'Time management was not kept; time was very limited to discuss issues.'
- 'Conference design papers were well prepared.'
- 'There were too many presenters; three to six presenters would have been adequate.
- 'The choice of the venue the conference was held in was well thought out.'
- 'Addressing the overall quality of the presentation, mental health needed to be addressed—depression, anxiety, and stress.'
- 'All performances of kids' poems were enjoyable and entertained members during long periods sitting.'
- 'More information about the Council of Elders (their objective and term) would have been better.'
- 'The unity of the community within the conference was enjoyable, as was bringing people together from overseas and meeting the people who have been separated from us for a long time.'
- 'It was good to evaluate our developmental program and what could be possible.'
- 'More information on the Australian system would have been desirable, as well as a more attractive research presentation.'

Overall, the conference was well received. However, there could have been improvements among the number and quality of the speakers, the content of the presentations, and the manner in which the conference was conducted in terms of time management

Appendix B) The Discussion Form

The Discussion With Help In Generating More Ideas About A Topic

1. Justify the choice of the issue (topic).
2. Frame the problem.
3. Identify whose behavior and what and how environmental factors need to change for the problem to begin to be solved.
4. Analyses the root causes of the problem.
5. Identify the restraining and driving forces that affect the problem. Forces retraining change here include:
6. Find any relationships that exist among the problem you are concerned with and others in the community. Forces restraining change here include:
7. Identify personal factors that may contribute to the problem. Some forces driving change might be.
8. Identify environmental factors that may contribute to the problem. Sample environmental factors:
9. Identify targets and agents of change for addressing the problem.

Targets of change might include:

A short list of potential agents of change:

Proposals

The purpose of compiling these discussion papers was to combine ideas from participants in the conference. This is a compilation of the topics and ideas that were discussed during the September event.

The Selection of Council of Elders Members
There will be five members chosen. In order to make this process less problematic, we will need to ensure that one member is elected from each state in which there is a Twi East association. By ensuring this, the association will have the best opportunity to engage with issues that are present across the nation. The association does not want to take a one-size-fits-all approach and risk creating problems of self-interest, ethnocentricity, ignorance, and policy that disproportionately affect certain groups.

Significant Day
It is of vital importance that the Twi East Community celebrates significant days. For example, Dr John Garang Day; Garang is one of our sons and leading liberators and should be celebrated as a freedom fighter. Celebrations of significant days will allow us to ensure that Twi East youth remember the sacrifices that were made for us in the past.

Education in Twi East Mainland
Education is a crucial factor of development. It would benefit the people of Twi East immensely if we helped to increase literacy. A fundamental issue with this is that, though there are numerous primary schools, there is only one secondary school in the area.

In order to alleviate this problem, people need to commit to building secondary schools in the Twi East mainland area. Current barriers to this are a lack of resources, a lack of investment, and ignorance to the value of education. We can overcome these issues by promoting awareness of education as a priority. The potential agents of this change include NGOs from South Sudan and Australia, the Twi East community, and the South Sudanese Government.

Development
This topic is about social, economic, and political development, which all require effective social inclusion and unity. Factors that hinder this development include lack of personal development, misconceptions about the Twi East association, a lack of knowledge about the constitution, and illiteracy. All of these result from distrust and miscommunication. The core environmental factor at play here is Western society. The way forward needs to be paved with peace and reconciliation, open dialogue, professional development, community engagement, and youth program support.

Twi East Community Priorities
There are many challenges facing Twi people, and all of these require rapid response by leadership. The core priority for the Twi East community in South Sudan is the security of its citizens.

Health and Wellbeing
Many attendees were interested to hear more about the topic of health and wellbeing, particularly relating to mental health.

Road Safety
There were stronger suggestions about road safety initiatives that could help to improve security in Twi East.

Hopefully, in the future, we can have more engagement and discussion on the topics mentioned above and other issues in our community.

Appendix C) Attendance Lists

S/No	Name in Full	Sex	State
1	Deng Chol Riak	M	Qld
2	Garang Juac Theiu	M	ACT
3	Ayiik Chol Anyang	M	Vic
4	Akoi Bol Nyuon	M	Vic
5	Mamer Yaak Dut	M	SA
6	Majok Lual Deng	M	NT
7	Garang Deng Aleu	M	NSW
8	Garang Deng Gak	M	SA
9	Galou Mayen Mabior	M	VIC
10	David Dau Deng	M	ACT
11	Bul Duom Bul	M	VIC
12	Adoor Akechnhial Adoor	M	Vic
13	Bol Kut Garang	M	Vic
14	Ayiik Chol Deng	M	Vic
15	Lual Akoi Deng	M	WA
16	Akol Dhiak Akol	M	Vic
17	Ayuen Kuereng Yai	M	Vic
18	Ayuen Biar Atem	M	Vic
19	Arok Aleu Arok	M	Vic
20	Atem Ajak Mabior	M	Vic
21	Atem Machar Atem	M	Vic
22	Garang Dhieu Dau	M	Vic
23	Lual Garang Dut	M	Vic
24	Abany Monykuch Bior	M	Vic
25	Makuei Koor Makuei	M	Vic
26	Chut Aleer Chut	M	ACT
27	Garang Kuir Mayen	M	Vic
28	Deng Garang Malual	M	Vic
29	Mabior Atem Duom	M	Vic
30	Mathiang Garang Piok	M	Qld
31	Mawut Chol Akoi	M	Vic
32	Geu Arok Gak	M	Vic
33	Bol Amol Tuol	M	SA
34	Aweng Mayom Aweng	M	Qld
35	Gai Biar Aweng	M	Vic
36	Thon Mayom Koor	M	Vic
37	Ajang Alaak Yuot	M	SA
38	Biar Kuek Atem	M	Vic
39	Malual Chol Deng	M	Vic
40	Atem Aluong Gak	M	WA
41	Awan Kuol Awan	M	Vic
42	Abraham Deng Michael	M	NSW
43	Makuei Dau Kuir	M	Vic
44	Manyok Kuany Deng	M	SA
45	Jacob Arok Chol	M	Vic
46	James Atem Mayen	M	Vic
47	Ajieth Atem Ajieth	M	SA
48	Ajang Pager Alaak	M	SA
49	Ayen William	F	Vic
50	Yar Dau Angok	F	Vic
51	Garang Mayen Kuol	M	Vic
52	Akech Dau Angok	M	WA
53	Dhiak Panther Thuch Dut	M	SA
54	Mayen Deng Ayii	M	Vic
55	John Dau Wach Deng	M	Qld
56	Simon Manyuon Atem	M	SA
57	Makuach Akech Arok	M	Vic
58	Alou Kuir Mabior	M	Vic
59	Lual Reech Deng	M	WA
60	Dual Ahou Dual	M	Vic
61	Mose Makuach Arok	M	Vic
62	Garang Kuer Bul	M	ACT
63	Ngang Ajang Chuoth		
64	Akech Ajang Achuoth	M	
65	Akol Maluk Chol	M	Vic
66	Adhieu Lual Nuul	M	Vic
67	Dual Malual	M	Vic
68	Deng Atem Aruel	M	Vic
69	Arok Atuil Atem	M	Vic
70	Adau Dut	M	Vic
71	Mary Agau Ajang	F	Vic
72	Ayen Chol Garang	F	Vic
73	Achol Kuol Dut	F	SA
74	Rebecca Bul	F	SA
75	Achol Garang Aguer	F	ACT
76	Anyakiir Aweng	F	Vic
77	Mayen Terry	M	Vic
78	Dut Juach	M	Vic
79	Majak Deng	M	NSW
80	David Makuach Piok	M	ACT
81	Apajok Yaak Dut	F	Vic
82	william Deng Manyok	M	ACT
83	Maliet Duot Aleer	M	ACT
84	Mabior Ajak Kuir Mayen	M	Vic
85	Adau Bior Deng	F	Vic

#	Name	Sex	State	#	Name	Sex	State
86	Athok Deng	F	Vic	137	Peter Manyok Kuot	M	ACT
87	Agau Deng Ajak	F		138	Gabriel Pawuoi Mayen	M	Vic
88	Dau Mayom Biar	M	SA	139	Chol Kuir Rongdit	M	Vic
89	Garang Kuir Ayiik	M	Vic	140	Atem Mayen Kuol	M	Vic
90	Garang Deng Gak	M	Old/SA	141	Atemdit Dau	M	Vic
91	Jacob Deng Garang	M	Vic	142	Chol Mark Awer	M	Vic
92	Amer Manyok Mading	M	Vic	143	Majok Dhieu Dau	M	Vic
93	Deng Chier	M	Vic	144	Manyok Ajang Makuei	M	SA
94	Ajah Ajak Deng	M	Vic	145	Gaarang Dau Jhot	M	NSW
95	Mabior Nyuon Deng	M	ACT	146	Nuul Mayen Deng	M	NSW
96	Deng Ajak	M		147	Daniel Mayen Lual	M	Qld
97	Gai Dau Majak	M	SA	148	Dhieu Mayen Dhieu	M	ACT
98	Biar Ajang Garang	M	SA	149	Anyieth Dau Angoth	M	Qld
99	Deng Ajang Duot	M	ACT	150	Lual Mayen Dhieu	M	ACT
100	Atem Dhieu Garang	M	ACT	151	Riak Garang Deng	F	Vic
101	Achol Majak Kuol	F	Vic	152	Athok Majok Kuany	F	Qld
102	Nyandeng Malual	F	Vic	153	Makuach Deng Gak	M	Vic
103	Deng Lueth Deng	M	NSW	154	Deng Jurkuch	M	Qld
104	Garang Manyang Duot	M	SA	155	Samuel Khot Majok	M	Nsw
105	James Chol Padiet	M	Vic	156	Daniel Mabior Amol	M	SA
106	Manyok Ajak Mabil	M	SA	157	Barach Chol Dau	M	Qld
107	Manyok Arok Duot	M	ACT	158	Garang Bol Ajang	M	NSW
108	Simon Mabior Mabil	M	SA	159	Chol Jurkuch Barach	M	SS
109	Bul Manyok Duot	M	VIC	160	Gak Deng Gak	M	Vic
110	Manyok Maketh Mading	M	VIC	161	Aguer Dut Ajang	F	Vic
111	John Adoor Deng	M	Qld	162	Sarah Ateng Maluk	F	Vic
112	Kon Atem Gak	M	SA	163	Redher Akuach Nipo	F	Vic
113	Majok Ajith Deng	M	SA	164	Kuany Deng Barach	F	Vic
114	Kuol Dhieu Ajang	M	SA	165	Philip Aguer Panyang	M	SS
115	Deng Mayen Ajang	M	Vic	166	Ayuel Gak Panyang	M	Vic
116	Ajak Manyok Deng	M	Vic	167	Ayiik Chol Deng	M	Vic
117	Chol Akech Ajak	M	SA	168	Makual Dut Yaak	M	Vic
118	Lual Akech Lual	M	Vic	169	Abuk Deng Agok	F	Vic
119	Garang Isaac Pantheer	M	Vic	170	Deng Garang Reech	M	Vic
120	Deng wal Deng	M	Vic	171	Panther Garang Dut	M	SA
121	Duot Manyang Kut	M	Vic	172	Philip Ajak Kon	M	Vic
122	Demg Amol Dau	M	Vic	173	Peter Mabior Kon	M	Vic
123	Bol Ador Deng	M	ACT	174	Abraham Juach Lueth	M	SA
124	Garang Mayen Atem	M	NSW	175	Andrew Mayen Kuol	M	
125	Biar Malual Atem	M	NSW	176	Michael Matiop Dau	M	SA
126	Samwuel Deng Akuei	M	Vic	177	Kuir Deng Kuir	M	Vic
127	Reech Garang Reech	M	Vic	178	Deng Bul Koch	M	Vic
128	Reech Kongor Gak	M	Vic	179	Chol Majok Chol	M	WA
129	Dhiak Akol Mabior	M	Qld	180	David Makuch Piok.	M	ACT
130	Diing Bul Atem	M	NSW	181	James Mading Mabil	M	NSW
131	Ador Akechnhial Ador	M	Vic	182	Gabriel Atem Wal	M	Vic
132	Alaak Duot Pageer	M	ACT	183	Akuol Mabior Makuol	F	Vic
133	Ajak Ayiei Manyok	M	Vic	184	Bol ngang	M	NSW
134	Jaba Ajang Bior	M	SA	185	Deng Dau Deng	M	Vic
135	Abel Atem Kuany	M	Vic	186	Deng Thon Jot	M	ACT
136	Gabriel Atem Lueth	M	SA	189	Deng Jok Diing	M	Vic

#	Name	Sex	State	#	Name	Sex	State
190	Dhieu Maluk	M	SA	241	Lual Deng Garang	M	
191	Jurkuch Deng AKuoch	M	Vic	242	Lual Dau Deng	M	
192	Diing Aruai Bol	M	Vic	243	Aluel Chol Kuir	F	Vic
193	Atem Yaak Atem	M	NSW	244	Kuei Thon Ngang	F	Vic
194	Isaiah Chol Aruai	M	SS	245	Malang Ajang Arok	F	Vic
195	Majok Ajieth Deng	M	SA	246	Achol Deng Gak	F	SA
196	Deng Mading Mayen	M		247	Bior Aguer Kuer	M	ACT
197	Deng Chiman Garang	M	Vic	248	Ajang Padiet	M	ACT
198	Garang Deng Yiyieth	M	SA	249	David yout Ajang	M	SA
199	Ajang Kiir Achien	M	SA	250	Majok Atem	M	Vic
200	John Deng Mabior	M	Vic	251	Pajok Arok Duot	M	Vic
201	Thiong Akech Atem	M	Vic	252	Mayen Thiak Lueth	M	Vic
202	Chol Garang Atem	M	Vic	253	Thuch Atem Marier	M	SA
203	Mabior Malual Deng	M		254	Peter Mabior Achuoth	M	Vic
204	Deng Akoi Deng	M		255	Priscilla Deng Jurkuch	F	Qld
205	Akech Manyang Deng	F	Vic	256	Tabitha Adol Kuir	F	Vic
206	Atem Akoi Deng	M		257	Adut Ajuong Kuir	F	Vic
207	Deng Garang Atem	M	Vic	258	Akuk Maper Beek		
208	Mary Aweng Ajang	F		259	Goch Dut Goch	M	Vic
209	Chol Arok Gak	M	VIC	260	Marol Manyang Kut	M	Vic
210	Garang Deng Garang	M	VIC	261	Anyuon Manyok Thiak	M	Vic
211	Dut Biar Manyuon	M	SA	262	Majok Atem Garang Beny	M	VIC
212	Akech Mayen Mading	F	VIC	263	Dut Kuot Mabior	M	Vic
213	Nyanwut Makuur	F		264	Mabior Kuot Mabior	M	Vic
214	Aguin Makuach Aguin	M	Qld	265	Kuot M Kuot	M	Vic
215	Akol Dau Chawuoch	M	Vic	266	Adhieu Aleu	F	Vic
216	Awien Chol Deng	M	Qld	267	Mark Aguer Atem	M	Vic
217	Majak Jawat Malek	M	WA	268	Kon Mabior Gak	M	SA
218	Daniel Makuei Jok	M		269	Garang Dhieu Dau	M	Vic
219	Adut Madiing Geu	F	Vic	270	Bol Aruai Yaak	M	Vic
220	Apiu Anok Yuang	F	Vic	271	Chol Akech Nyieth	M	Vic
221	Aruai Deng Gak	M	Vic	272	Biar Manyok Akech	M	Vic
222	Agoot Kuany Arok	M	Vic	273	Chol Garang Atem	M	Vic
223	Abiei Mabil Awer	F	Vic	274	Achol Aleu Atem	F	Vic
224	Adhieu Chol Bior	F	Vic	275	Nyakiir Majok Chol	F	Vic
225	Chol Aweng	M		276	Nyankuer Akuein Nul	F	
226	Kelei Deng Biar	M	ACT	277	Adhieu Akuein Nul	F	
227	Aker Chol	F	Vic	278	Nul Akuein Nul	M	
228	Achol Machar Atem	F	Vic	279	Kon Akuein Nul	F	
229	Ajak Maker	M	Vic	300	Abuk Dut	F	
230	Matiop Ajak	M	Vic	301	Nyanjur Garang Kuot	F	Vic
231	Akech Atem Gak	M	Vic	302	Aguer Paul Bol Kuir	M	SS
232	Ajang John	M	NSW	303	Jacob Lem Ziak	M	Vic
233	Aleer Garang Deng	M	ACT	304	Chol Malek Ajok	M	
234	Nuul Chol Deng	M	NSW	305	Apajok Deng Biar	F	Vic
235	Wel Chol Kuir	M	ACT	306	Achol Mayen Mabior	F	Vic
236	Majak Kuek Biar	M	NSW	307	RiaL Kuol Jok	F	Vic
237	Riak Garang Atem	M		308	Martha Tor	F	Vic
238	Akol Garang Malual	M	Vic	309	Emmuel Anyang Majok	M	Vic
239	Deng Lual Denuon	M	Vic	310	Dhieu Deng Barach	M	Vic
240	Bol Nul Dhieu	M	Vic	311	Yar Garang Deng	F	

#	Name	Sex	State	#	Name	Sex	State
312	Chol Ayiik Goch	M	Vic	363	Akech Majok	F	Vic
313	Ayom Ajiu	M	Vic	364	Asunta Majur	F	Vic
314	Alek Guot	M	Vic	365	Achol Maker Deng	F	Vic
315	Ator Chol Ayiik	M	Vic	366	Aluel Bior Kuir	F	Vic
316	Goch Chol Ayiik	M	Vic	367	Adum Garang	F	Vic
317	Adhieu Chol	F	Vic	368	Achol Bior Atem	F	Vic
318	Manya Deng Dau	M	WA	369	Jacob Chol Deng	M	NSW
319	Elizabeth Majok	F	Vic	370	Jacob Mabior Mabil	M	ACT
320	Hakima Majok	F	Vic	371	Deng Adoor Deng	M	ACT
321	Yar Garang	F	Vic	372	Akur Jok Deng	F	ACT
322	Kuir Thon Atem	F	NSW	373	Apajok Abit	F	Vic
323	Arok Dut	M		374	Ayor	F	
324	Manyok Juac Duot	M	Vic	375	Dabora	F	
325	Aguer			376	Atem Kuir Atem	M	
326	Awak Ajang Duot	F	Vic	377	Nyankiir Deng Akuach	F	Vic
327	Nyaret	F	Vic	378	Abuk Thuch Ajak	F	Vic
328	Chol Macher	M	Vic	379	Awek Bol Akech	F	Vic
329	Ader Kuir			380	Adit Ngon Deng	F	Vic
330	Nyabol Kuany Chol	F	Vic	381	Abiol Ajak Acuek Lual	F	Vic
331	Achol Ajok	F		382	Rebecca Ayen Achuoth	F	Vic
332	Atem Garang Atem	M	VIC	383	Tina Arok Mayom Deng	F	Vic
333	Barach Garang Atem	M	Vic	384	Arok Garang Dut	F	Vic
334	Atem Manyang Atem	M		385	Adau Wach Kuol	F	Vic
335	Malang Garang Atem	M		386	Aker Majok Tuil	F	Vic
336	Kongor Maketh Gak	M	Vic	387	Rabecca Ayen Lil	F	Vic
337	Achol Kongor Gak	F	Vic	388	Awak Chol Kuany	F	Vic
338	Abeny Kucha	F	SA	389	Awier Jok	F	Vic
339	Eshraga G Barbari	F	Vic	390	Saphano Deng Ajang	M	Vic
340	Warabek Ayuel	M	Vic	391	Nyankor Ador	F	ACT
341	Mabior Abit Biar	M	Vic	392	Jeremy Akoy Deng	M	ACT
342	Ajak Deng Ajak	M		393	Aguet Aguer Bookiei	F	ACT
343	Daniel Atuek Mabior	M		394	Biar Arok	M	Vic
344	Elizabeth Nyakuot Agok	F		395	Deng Kuek	M	Vic
345	Monica Kuany Agook	F		396	Majok Deng Garang	M	Vic
346	Kongor Arok Reg	M		397	Ngok Deng	F	Vic
347	Reech Amol	M		398	Deng Dau Deng	M	Vic
348	Mabior Deng Mabior	M	Vic	399	Yar Ngong Aluong	F	Vic
349	Ajak Amol	M		400	Khot Deng Bul	F	Vic
350	Deng Ajak Deng Biar	M		401	Ayen Atem	F	Vic
351	Mabior Abit Biar	M	Vic	402	Kuir Gak	F	Vic
352	Rebecca Mayen	F	ACT	403	Adit Atem	F	
353	Mary Awach	F		404	Adhieu Duot	F	Vic
354	Margaret Chuol	F		405	Aluel Bol	F	Vic
355	Duom Bol Kunjok	F	Vic	406	Deng Garang Reech	M	Vic
356	Nyijur Chol Deng	F	Vic	407	Maketh Chol	M	Vic
357	Amer Diing	F	Vic	408	Nyandeng Pawach	F	Vic
358	Abuk Chol	F	Vic	409	Nyakiir Deng Akuoch	F	Vic
359	Abuol Mayen	F	Vic	410	Yar Dau	F	Vic
360	Achok Majok Dut	F	Vic	411	Abuk Manyuon	F	Vic
361	Rachel Agok Biar	F	Vic	412	Yar Garang	F	Vic
362	Alek Kuany Chol	F	Vic	413	Nul Deng Garang	M	Vic

414	Lual Chol Kuir	M	Vic
415	Yar Kuer Kuir	F	
516	Akur Maper Beek	F	Vic
517	Dut Dhieu Dut	M	Vic
518	Ajak Dhieu Dut	M	Vic
519	Athieng Garang Chol	F	Vic
520	David Duot	M	Vic
521	Adhieu Thuch	F	ACT
522	Akuol Bul	F	ACT
523	Adau Gak	F	Vic
524	Ayuen Bol Maketh	F	Vic
525	Bul Garang Atem	M	Vic
526	Simon Akech Achuoth	M	Qld
527	Majok Jawat	M	WA
528	Abuk Awai	F	Vic
529	Manyang Biar Kuir	M	SA
530	Pajok Arok Deng	M	ACT
531	Achol Atem Nyok	F	Vic
531	Athieng Kuereng Angok	F	Vic
532	Anyien Achien Gak	F	Vic
533	Anyier Jok Akol	F	Vic
534	Arok Ayiik Goch	F	Vic
535	Yar Dau Dhieu	F	Vic
536	Adier Garang Deng	F	Vic
537	Abuk Deng Wal	F	Vic
538	Akuot Makuei Dau	F	Vic
539	Aker Ajak	F	Vic
540	Aluel Goch	F	Vic
541	Nyankiir Chol	F	Vic
542	Elizabeth Aheu Deng	F	Vic
543	Deng Jang Awach	M	WA
544	Abraham Chol Lual	M	NSW
545	Kuer Dau Apai	M	NSW
546	Chol Achuoth Ajang	M	NSW
547	Deng Atem Ruel	M	NSW
548	Atem Kuir Atem	M	NSW
549	Bul Yak Dau	M	Vic

Appendix D) The Conference Research Paper Processes

Stage	Items	Action by	Deadline	Remarks
01	Allocation of the topics	TECAA	10.08.19	Done
02	Submission of the draft paper to the TECAA for Conference purposes.	Researcher	16.09.19	Done
03	Printing of the drafts.	TECAA	18.09.19	Done
04	Presenting fact-findings and handing out of the draft copies to the attendees.	Researcher/Presenter	21.09.19	Done
05	Handing out of the questionaries' to the participants/attendees.	Researcher	21.09.19	Done
06	Collection of the questionnaire copies back to the researcher/presenter for final compilation.	TECAA	21.09.19	Done
07	Adding in of the new information found from questionaries' to the research paper	Researcher	15.10.19	Done
08	Summarization of the information into a final document	Researcher/Editors	21.12.19	Done
09	Submission of the final paper to TECAA-EMC	Researcher	22.12.19	Done
10	Printing of the final copy of the document	TECAA-EMC/Printer	10.02.20	Done
11	Final Report to TECAA	EMC	22.03.20	Done
12	Supplying the final document to stakeholders (States and Payam Leaders) (globally) for their record keeping.	TECAA	30.03.20	Done
13	Implementing the programs	TECAA + Community	2020	

Appendix E) Name Tag Policy

Dear Leaders and Members,

Here are policies, responsibilities and procedures for wearing name tag during the conference days.
- Three names and title are requested to print your name tag.
- Name tags are picked up upon arrival when you check in at the registration desk. Small pin worn on jacket and attached to bag.
- Make sure your lanyards are adjustable to avoid awkward positioning.
- To identify attendees by their names for security reasons and insurance policy.
- TECAA-EMC requires all attendees to wear their name tag at all times during conference hours. To facilitate making new connections.
- Meeting other people and call by their name.
- Everyone must be wearing a name tag, no exception.
- Should you lose your name tag, please come back to the registration desk to receive a replacement?
- Don't put it in your pocket.9
- Don't leave it behind on the table or at home.
- Don't take it off when you go outside for smoking.

All information provided will be treated confidentially and for TECAA policy.

The TECAA- EMC considered the name tag as important networking tool, to help identified attendees and meet other policies requirements.

Thank you to prioritize serving your community in your busy schedule. Please, should you have any queries about these procedures, don't hesitate to contact us on Twiommunityassociation- aus@outlook.com.

Appendix F) The Order Of Proceedings In The Event Proceedings

(Day 1) (2hrs) Part (A) Agm

Time	Activities	Who is Responsible
	Attendees obtain Name tag at Registration Desk	
(10mins)	Program opening with Prayers	Pastor (TBA)
(05mins)	Housekeeping by the Master of Ceremony (MC)	Ayiik & Akoi
(05mins)	Welcoming message by the Host State	Akol Dhiak Akol
(07mins)	Introduction of the VIPs and Invited Guests	Gabriel Garang Juach
(30mins)	TECAA President Speech about the Association	Deng Chol Riak
(10mins)	Remarks from member of the Council of Elders	Gum Akech
(30mins)	Resolutions	

Part (B) Conference Proceedings (3hrs)

Time	Topic	Presenter
(10mins)	Conference papers distributed and highlighted the purpose and desired outcomes	David Dau Deng
(15mins)	Concurrent presentation: Org. Function Review	Garang Deng and Deng Amol
(15mins)	Concurrent Presentation: Health and Wellbeing	Garang Kuir Ayiik
(15mins)	Concurrent Presentation: Sociocultural	Atem Yaak Atem
(15mins)	Concurrent Presentation: Education	Mecak Ajang Alaak
(20mins)	Resolutions	
	Collecting Questionnaires	

Part (C) Keynote Speakers (4hrs)

Time	Order of Speakers	Who is Responsible
(05mins)	Representative for Payam Leaders	Thuch Atem
(05mins)	Representative for States/Territories' Leaders	Majok Jawac Malek
(05mins)	Chairman of Jieng Council in Victoria	TBA
(05mins)	South Sudanese Leadership in Victoria	Akol Dhiak Akol
(06mins)	Bor Community in Australia	TBA
(05mins)	Duken community in Australia	TBA
(05mins)	Twi East Women Affairs	Ayen Garang Dut
(05mins)	Twi East Youth Affairs	Chol Akech Ajak
(05mins)	TECAA Former President	Kuer Dau Apach
(1.5hrs)	VIPS Delivers Speech • Youth Chairman (10mins) • Member of Invited Guests (10mins) • On behalf of Intellectual (10mins) • On behalf of Twi East at home (15mins) • On behalf of Twi East of Australia (10mins) • Guest of Honor (30mins) • Pastor	Diing Ajang Awuol Ayiei Manyok Ajak Kuir Dau-thii Isaiah Chol Aruai Bul Duop Former Governor Mark Atem Thuch
	Evaluation form return and closing Day 1 program	

Part (D) Other Business (OB) (DAY 2)

Time	Activities	Who is Responsible
	Prayers	TBA
	Welcome and Opening Remarks	TBA
	General Q and A (Interactions)	TBA
	Donations / in-kind Contribution	TBA
	Announcements	TBA
	Closing Remarks	TBA
	TECAA wrap up event	TBA
	Youth activities (Bul/Loor)	TBA
	Conference Closing	TBA

Appendix G) TECAA Invitation Letter

We are pleased to invite you and members of your organization to attend the TECAA2019 Reunion Conference as that is being organized by TECAA Inc1601085 under the **THEMES: NEW APPROACH + NEW IDEAS = SUPPORTING PROGRESS**. The conference will be run for two days from 21 to 22 the September 2019. We wish members to be in Melbourne by 20th of Sept 2019.

Three Key Objectives For This Conference:
- To engage on the issue of how Twi East Community participants across disciplines can be better involved in policy formulation and development by sharing global experiences on knowledge co-production and other methodologies. Also, to offer a platform for learning and developing new ways to engage in community.
- To provide interactive avenues for a debate and knowledge transfer that shall give policy makers, planners and practitioners in general the opportunity to learn about current contribution from this conference.
- To engage in preliminary dialogue on the ways in which spatial, social and economic inequality are addressed within the framework of the new Twi East Community big agenda and translated in policy spaces across the globe. Also, shall provide a unique opportunity for new working link that would be established to facilitate cooperation amongst the Twi East members.

The diverse participation will enable a robust knowledge sharing and time for reflection on new ways to strengthen policy responses in line with the new Twi East Community big agenda.

Your response to attend will be greatly appreciated. If you require any further information regarding this invitation, please do not hesitate to contact Event Management Committee (EMC) on email Twiommunityassociation-aus@outlook.com

Appendix H) Appreciation Letter

To presenters, performers, organisers, participates, and invited guests for their outstanding contribution toward the succeed of 2019 conference. I would like to take this opportunity to express my heartfelt thanks to you for your very active participation in our TECAA2019-AGM/Reunion Conference just concluded at the Sunday in Melbourne. The President and executives have also asked me to pass on their sincere appreciation for your efforts in supporting the Conference in this important undertaking topic.

Your skills in talking about different approaches of the Twi East Conference were highly appreciated by those representing all sides of that extremely sensitive topic. We have also received numerous phone calls from community members to register their appreciation on your contributions. It appears that you may have confined useful information to benefit our Association.

Please accept our appreciation for such admirable job. We will take your words into practice. You have covered more essential elements of community development and your description of how to execute it is remarkable and we are looking forward to work together on Phase II.

I once again would like to thank you for such a wonderful presentation, and again for making time in your busy schedule to attend the Twi East Conference and make a heartfelt contribution.

TECAA 2019-REUNION CONFERENCE IN MELBOURNE.

NEW APPROACH + NEW IDEAS = SUPPORTING PROGRESS

THE 3 KEY OBJECTIVES OF THE CONFERENCE

KEY ONE
TO ENGAGE ON THE ISSUE OF HOW TECCA PARTICIPANTS ACROSS DISCIPLINES CAN BE BETTER INVOLVED IN POLICY FORMULATION AND DEVELOPMENT BY SHARING GLOBAL EXPERIENCES ON KNOWLEDGE CO-PRODUCTION AND OTHER METHODOLOGIES. ALSO, TO OFFER A PLATFORM FOR LEARNING AND DEVELOPING NEW WAYS TO ENGAGE IN COMMUNITY.

KEY TWO
TO PROVIDE INTERACTIVE AVENUES FOR A DEBATE AND KNOWLEDGE TRANSFER THAT SHALL GIVE POLICY MAKERS, PLANNERS AND PRACTITIONERS IN GENERAL THE OPPORTUNITY TO LEARN ABOUT CURRENT CONTRIBUTION FROM THIS CONFERENCE.

KEY THREE
TO ENGAGE IN PRELIMINARY DIALOGUE ON THE WAYS IN WHICH SPATIAL, SOCIAL AND ECONOMIC INEQUALITY ARE ADDRESSED WITHIN THE FRAMEWORK OF THE NEW TECCA AGENDA AND TRANSLATED IN POLICY SPACES ACROSS THE GLOBE. ALSO, SHALL PROVIDE A UNIQUE OPPORTUNITY FOR NEW WORKING LINK THAT WOULD BE ESTABLISHED TO FACILITATE COOPERATION AMONGST THE TWI EAST MEMBERS.

TECAA CULTURE

WE, THE PEOPLE OF THIS ORGANISATION ARE MUCH AWARE OF THE FACT THAT UNLESS WE ORGANISE AND SUPPORT OURSELVES UNDER ONE FEDERAL BODY, OUR PARTICIPATION AND CONTRIBUTION IN ACHIEVING COMMON GOALS AND WELFARE OF TWI COMMUNITY IN AUSTRALIA AND OVERSEAS WOULD BE MINIMAL. THE RECOGNITION OF SUCH ASPIRATIONS LED TO THE ESTABLISHMENT OF TWI EAST COMMUNITY ASSOCIATION OF AUSTRALIA TO CREATE STRONG AND PROPER COMMUNITY STRUCTURES AND NETWORKS AMONGST MEMBERS OF THIS ORGANISATION

WHILE GRATEFUL TO THE AUSTRALIAN GOVERNMENT FOR ACCORDING RESETTLEMENT TO THE SOUTH SUDANESE IN AUSTRALIA, THE MEMBERS OF THIS ORGANISATION WILL CONTINUE TO POSITIVELY INTERACT AND ENGAGE WITH THE AUSTRALIAN SOCIETY AND THEIR GOVERNMENTS TO ACHIEVE COMMON GOALS.

TO ACHIEVE THIS MISSION, THIS ORGANISATION WILL REPRESENT AND ADVANCE THE WELFARE AND INTERESTS OF ITS MEMBERS THROUGH ITS EXECUTIVE COMMITTEE AND IN COORDINATION AND WORKING IN PARTNERSHIP WITH RELATED ASSOCIATIONS TO ENHANCE GREATER COOPERATION AT FEDERAL LEVEL. THE ASSOCIATION WILL ALSO CO-OPERATE WITH THE REST OF COMMUNITY MEMBERS ACROSS THE WORLD IN ORDER TO PROTECT AND DEFEND TWI COMMUNITY INTEREST

WELCOME TO MELBOURNE - VICTORIA

Twi East Members Waiting for the Conference to Start

TWI EAST MEMBERS FOR REUNION

MELBOURNE 2019

Arrival & Welcoming of Delegates

www.ingramcontent.com/pod-product-compliance
Lightning Source LLC
Chambersburg PA
CBHW041711290426
44109CB00028B/2846